THE TEN COMMANDMENTS FOR GRANDPARENTS

*A Wise and Witty Handbook
for Today's Grandmas and Grandpas*

CARYL WALLER KRUEGER

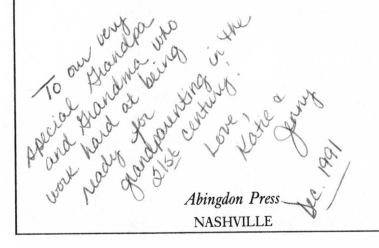

To our very
special Grandpa
and Grandma who
work hard at being
ready for
grandparenting in the
21st century.
Love,
Katie &
Jenny
Dec. 1991

Abingdon Press
NASHVILLE

THE TEN COMMANDMENTS FOR GRANDPARENTS

Copyright © 1991 by Caryl W. Krueger

This book is printed on acid-free paper.

Library of Congress Cataloging-in-Publication Data

KRUEGER, CARYL WALLER, 1929-
  The ten commandments for grandparents: a wise and witty handbook for today's grandmas and grandpas / Caryl Waller Krueger.
     p.   cm.
  Includes bibliographical references and index.
  ISBN 0-687-41237-4 (pbk. : alk. paper)
  1. Grandparenting—United States. 2. Grandparent and child—United States.   I. Title.
  HQ759.9.K78   1991
  306.874'5—dc20   90-22423
                                                                        CIP

The author has made every effort to make the information and suggestions in this book practical and workable, but neither she nor the publisher assumes any responsibility for successes, failures, or other results of putting these ideas into practice.

MANUFACTURED IN THE UNITED STATES OF AMERICA

To Elieth

who exemplifies the perfect grandmother! She nurtures her grandchildren from the day they are born and onward in their young lives without intruding on the prerogatives of the parents. At the same time, she encourages the individuality of her own children and their spouses, enfolding them in her love. And along with her many civic and church contributions, she still enjoys a full and rewarding life with her husband.

Other books by Caryl Krueger:

Working Parent—Happy Child (Abingdon Press, 1990)
1001 Things to Do with Your Kids (Abingdon Press, 1988)
Six Weeks to Better Parenting (Pelican Publishers, 1985)

Acknowledgments

Hundreds of grandparents in the United States and Canada contributed to the ideas and statistics in this book. I'm also grateful for the more than two thousand grandchildren they spoke of with love and pride. Without these children, the book would have been mere theory rather than one with workable, tested ideas. Others who helped me include several very wise great-grandparents who shared their expertise from a long-range view of family life. And, as always, I appreciate the input of Sheila Kinder and Cliff Krueger, who read and shared ideas on the manuscript.

Your grand job . . .

So you're a grandparent! Now comes the fun. You've done your best at being a parent and raising your own family. Now you can watch how the next generation does it!

Unless you choose to get involved (or unusual conditions force your involvement), you no longer have those middle-of-the-night baby feedings, those sessions supervising homework, those midnight watches until the teens are all home safely, or those big college bills to pay.

But that doesn't mean you don't have an essential job. The grand job of grandparenting is a supportive and vital one. There are creative, educational, and enjoyable things for you to do, and you can choose just how involved you want to be.

Our mobile world, with families often living great distances from relatives, sometimes requires us to make a little extra effort to make an impact as a grandparent. But this connection between the generations is important for the survival of the family. So whether your grandchild is next door or across the ocean, there are interesting and essential things for you to do. *That's what this book is about: grand things for grandparents to do.*

Centuries ago, the rules for living were set down in the Ten Commandments—and these rules brought their followers through the wilderness. Today, there is a new form of wilderness. It is the crumbling concept of family in a rapidly changing society. While this book is not one of religious doctrine, its Ten Commandments can bring new joys to family living and enrich child, parent, and grandparent, thus strengthening the family as the very foundation of life.

The word *grand* means magnificent, splendid, of great importance. That's you! Now read on about your grand job.

Caryl Waller Krueger

Contents

One

THE FIRST COMMANDMENT:

You shall communicate energetically with your grandchildren

Dear Grandma,

Our three grandchildren are thirteen, six, and four years of age, and we do a fair job of keeping in touch. It's easy when they're small, but as they get older, we feel more distant. Kristin, the teenager, almost seems like a stranger now, yet we were so close when she was in grade school. Is this just "the way it has to be"?

WONDERING GRANDPARENTS

You aren't the only wondering grandparents! How to keep in touch from baby to toddler to teen to grown-up is one of the most difficult aspects of grandparenting—especially if you don't live nearby.

When it comes to good communication, there isn't just one good way to achieve it. It varies with the ages of the grandchildren, and it varies with their personalities and environments.

Grandparents themselves have changed, too. They aren't as they are often pictured: a sweet, gray-haired couple drinking lemonade while sitting in rocking chairs on the porch. They are former flower children, bobby soxers, and Beatlemaniacs.

And with the increase in longevity, today's grandparents have careers and active lives of their own. They probably don't live just around the corner, and the highlight of their week *isn't* serving chicken dinner to the family every Sunday! Often, they're both busy with jobs and civic activities. They also may sit on a board of directors, run a tractor, play tennis and golf, and enjoy a day at Disneyland without any kids along.

So the rules have changed, but the need to communicate is still present.

Why Communicate?

The benefits of a close relationship among the three generations are many. Good communication brings family members closer together and at the same time promotes acceptance, appreciation, and understanding.

Good communication adds stability to the lives of the participants and contributes to self-esteem. It provides another comforting family tie in unsettled times, and it can be an oasis for solving problems.

Your own personal communication with grandchildren can enhance values, increase tolerance, overcome obstacles, and educate. And, at the top of the list, good communication between grandparent and grandchild reinforces the bonds of love.

This communication can and should be a joyful activity—the eager sharing of news, dreams, and love. It also is important as an outlet for our innermost feelings.

Simply put, communication results in a better life for both grandchild and grandparent.

When our children were young and we lived in Hawaii, their grandparents would come from the Mainland each year for a visit lasting about three weeks. While this was a very long time for three generations to be under one roof, it was a great improvement over the once-a-week/watch-your-manners/eat-and-run dinners we had had when living quite near to one another. At those polite dinners there was never enough time to really get to know each other under everyday circumstances.

However, during these three-week visits, there was great rapport, and the kids became very comfortable with their grandparents. Each one usually spoke his mind. We all recall this exchange between grandmother and five-year-old grandson:

Grandson: When are you going home, Grandma?
Grandma: Are you looking forward to our leaving?
Grandson: Maybe, but I want you to come back.
Grandma: Well, our plane leaves early tomorrow morning.
Grandson: Oh great, it's been so hard for me to be good for this long a time!

Grandma laughed and praised him for his good behavior, but she always loved to retell the story of being "encouraged" to leave!

How Well Do We Know Each Other?

If we're going to have vital conversations with our grandchildren, we have to know them—what things they like to do and what things they think about. We need a clear picture of the *individuality* of each grandchild. This is easier if you have only one or two grandchildren, harder when you have a whole bunch.

Getting one grandchild confused with another can be easy to do, but is embarrassing for the grandparent and annoying to the child. So you must remember which one plays soccer, which one detests fish, which one loves purple clothes, which one reads mystery books, and which one wants to be a veterinarian.

You need to keep these things in mind so that each conversation doesn't start back at box A with the question "What's new?" How much better to pick up where you left off with lines like: "How did the John LeCarré thriller turn out?" "What did you think of that fabulous goalie in the Soccer League play-offs?" (Note that these questions can't be answered just "yes" or "no," but require a more involved answer—an answer that can start a real conversation.)

One grandfather with ten grandchildren between the ages of five and ten years of age keeps a small black notebook. In it he has a page for each grandchild. He notes when he's called or written, what he's given in the way of gifts, and special facts about that grandchild—school grade, activities, special abilities. The grandchildren know he keeps his "little black book" and they even suggest things to put in it. Once one girl told him in April: "Write this down, Grandpa, in case I forget by Christmas: I really want a catcher's mitt." This is one grandpa who knows what's going on with his grandchildren!

Try this easy quiz to see how well you know your grandchildren. You may want to do it for each grandchild you have. Just answer "yes" or "no" to each question.

1. I know the name of my grandchild's current best friend.
2. I exchange pictures with my grandchild at least twice a year.
3. I am aware of my grandchild's latest achievements in school, sports, and other activities.
4. My grandchild knows what things I like to do.
5. I know my grandchild's favorite books and toys.
6. I see or communicate with my grandchild at least twice a month.
7. I have taken the time to share my feelings on values (honesty, responsibility, and so forth) with my grandchild.
8. My grandchild is helpful to me when we are together.
9. I am much more supportive than critical of the way my child is raising my grandchild.
10. In the last two weeks, I've told my grandchild how much I love him or her.

If you have nine or ten "yes" answers you're a grand grandparent. Six to eight shows you're doing well. But five or less—well, there's room for improvement!

Both grandmothers and grandfathers should take the quiz and compare answers. My research shows that while grandmas relate well to both sexes and all ages of grandchildren, grandpas often favor the males. They also spend more time with grade schoolers than with those children who are younger or older. These facts are urgent reminders to communicate with *all* grandchildren—starting when they're young—and to keep it up. All ages and both sexes of grandchildren need to feel that *both* grandparents care for them and need them.

Getting to really know your grandchild by sharing experiences, creating times for talk, and building memories together will make your communication much easier. Remember not to "talk down" to children—they recognize this so quickly. It's better to assume that they know more, rather than less. In fact, kids nowadays probably do.

Some Old, Some New Ways of Keeping in Touch

Of course, if you live next door, there's less of a problem finding the time to communicate. However, that communication may not be the best—it may be brief random comments as you wave across the backyard fence, rather than in-depth talk.

But today, the majority of grandparents live far away from their grandchildren and get-togethers are more apt to be monthly or even yearly. Even so communication with grandchildren is essential.

One-on-one, face-to-face talk is the best means of communicating. But here are other ways to keep in touch, starting with the more traditional:

1. The telephone. In an era of reaching out and touching others, this is the method most used by grandparents. Rather than just saying "hello" to a grandchild at the *end* of your conversation with your own child, specifically call and ask for the grandchild first. This makes her or him feel very important!

Here are a few other telephone twists:
* Tell grandchildren to call YOU collect once a month.
* Mark your calendar for special events in the life of a far-away grandchild. Then phone him or her the next day to ask about the play, game, or dance of the night before. Or phone the day before the event with your best wishes.
* Invite a nearby grandchild to come to your house, and together you can phone a distant cousin or friend.
* Drop pleasant hints in your conversation, such as, "I'm going to send you something in the mail this week" or "Let's each start a list of things we'll do together" or "You may be surprised with what I'm bringing along at Thanksgiving."
* Telephone collegiates on weeknights when they're more apt to be in their rooms studying. A short "love call" from you can be just the lift needed to be able to return to the books with new vigor.

2. The mail. Letter-writing is the second most popular way of communicating. Today's grandparents often write on typewriter or computer. In one case, a little girl commented on a postcard she received from her grandma: "Can you imagine, my card has real handwriting on it!"

Kids are very pleased to receive mail addressed to them, so look for occasions to communicate this way.
* Send cards, postcards, and hand-made greetings for every imaginable occasion: a birthday, Valentine's Day, the first day of spring, Easter, the last day of school, National Pickle Week, Independence Day, the first day of school, Halloween, and the first day of the exciting holiday month of December. Don't hesitate to invent your own holidays, so you have a reason to write.
* Postcards are great to send when you travel. Be sure your card makes a comment about the picture on the other side. Give grandchildren a shoe box with dividers for all fifty states and one for foreign countries. This will help them to start a postcard collection—and it can teach geography and history at the same time.

* Pretend you are a tourist in your own town. Go to a place where local postcards are sold and stock up on a variety. They are an inexpensive and interesting way to send a short message. One grandfather uses postcards of local attractions he's already visited with the grandchildren, or ones he plans to take them to on their next visit. Sometimes he uses a marking pen to draw himself and the youngsters into the picture he's sending. In one, he had them sitting inside the monkey cage at the zoo!

* For non-readers, write picture letters. You can send a message with a few simply drawn pictures.

* Give your grandchildren some notepaper with pre-addressed and stamped envelopes so that they can write privately to you. Make a writing kit (paper, envelopes, stamps, family addresses, and pen) to give a youngster away at camp or college.

* Send newspaper and magazine clippings that you think will interest your grandchild. Avoid "preachy" articles that might be construed as criticism of the youngster. One father felt so strongly about his collegiate children keeping in touch with the outside world that he started sending them a packet of interesting clippings each month. The clippings presented varied points of view and a wide range of topics. When friends and relatives heard about it, they wanted to be on the list, too. It's now ten years later and the list has grown to include three generations of readers. Some take the clippings on their commute, some read one a day, others read them aloud or at restaurants while waiting for the food to come. While many of the readers aren't related, it's still called "Uncle Cliff's Clipping Service." When the young set don't like a certain point of view, they're quick to tell him. They often send him clippings of their own liking for inclusion in the next month's packet. It's a great way of communicating!

* Sharing photographs. A grandmother always orders double prints of pictures she takes at home or when she visits

grandchildren. She doesn't immediately send the whole bunch because she knows that they'd be looked through quickly and laid aside. Instead, she wisely chooses one to send in each letter. She comments on her garden or dog, or reminds a child how much she enjoyed the picnic. She's also given the grandchildren the hint that they could keep these photos in their own personal photo album or scrapbook.

* Occasionally tuck other things in the envelope. One grandfather sends rose petals from his garden. A grandmother scents her letters with the tear-out samples of fragrances found in magazines. Another includes premiums or other freebies—calendars, plastic rulers, pens, pretty stickers.

3. Small visits and large celebrations. "Just dropping in" has "dropped out" of popularity in today's fast-paced life-style. Today the uninvited caller is frowned upon as someone who is usurping the family's free time. Grandparents may be at home awaiting an invitation—an invitation that often never comes.

Nowadays, families find little time for social events. Research shows that a typical working couple has a planned social event only about once a month. This can be sad for friends and relatives who feel left out, but it is even more sad for the husband/wife relationship that is devoid of both social occasions and private time spent together. Such a situation can occur when the couple's time is divided between work and kids, with no time for each other.

The easy-going get-togethers where conversation flowed and all the relatives felt like one big happy family do not happen as often today. Birthday and holiday gatherings and other celebrations sometimes get crammed into the schedule, and an entire chapter (chapter 5) shares ideas on how to make them meaningful and memorable.

For grandparents with families living nearby there is still need to plan visits: a weekend afternoon walk-and-talk . . . painting a child's room and having three-generation talk . . . lemonade in the shade and heart-to-heart talk. If relatives live near you, don't pass up this important time for communication and love. Visits do not need to take a long time—in fact, grandparents should always offer to make the visit brief, and leave it up to the parents to say "stay as long as you want." All three generations can benefit from the no-fuss visit.

4. Attending events together. Sometimes families need an event as a conveyor for conversation. An easy way to do this is to attend the same function: church, sports event, recital, concert. Some grandparents serve breakfast before church or brunch afterwards as a simple get-together. If you use this method, you must plan for important conversation "around" such events or during intermissions.

Many grandparents are eager to root for the school team (even when they lose) or applaud the bumblebee ballerina as she buzzes around the stage with ten similar insects. While many such events are free, there can be an occasional event that costs: a movie, symphony concert, or professional sports event.

I grew up in the Chicago area, which has the excellent Goodman Theatre downtown. From childhood through my early married years until my husband and I moved away, we attended six plays each year. My father had a block of second- and third-row seats, and grandparents, aunts, uncles, cousins, and other "almost-relatives" gathered at the theater well before curtain time to talk with one another. Then there was the hush of anticipation as the curtain rose. My mother often wondered if some of the themes were too mature for us, but we loved live theater and weren't easily shocked! There was always spirited conversation about the play during intermission, when my father would talk to each person as he passed the traditional box of candy. Then came the critiques shared en route home when all three generations gave their opinions. Some of those plays are in revival now, and, although I've seen them again, they haven't been as exhilarating as they were when I first viewed them with my cousin, whose favorite comment was "Oh my gosh—I gotta try that!"

There are countless other good occasions for communication among the generations: when grandparents babysit, on three-generation vacations, or when working on a project together. These will be covered in other chapters.

The Art of Communicating

Have you ever had a social evening with long blank pauses, an evening you couldn't wait to end? On the other hand, have you ever been to a party where the conversation was so fast and engaging that you wished it would go on forever? The difference between the two is usually the participants' abilities in the fine art of communication.

This is an easy-to-learn skill. In talking with grandchildren, many such skills come into play. Here are some suggestions to make intergenerational communication flow:

1. Listen as much as you talk. If there are four in the group, make sure you're not talking more than a quarter of the time.
2. Wait for a short pause before plunging in. Don't continually interrupt.
3. Don't be afraid of a short silence. Sometimes it's a sign that the others are thinking about what has been said. And some young people will talk only when they are sure the adults have finished. Avoid nervous, non-stop chattering.
4. Let the conversation flow freely. Don't be upset if it takes a turn away from your favorite topic. Don't try to mastermind the direction of the conversation.
5. When someone speaks at the same time you do, it is probably just eagerness to contribute. So be gracious and defer to the other person.
6. If the aim is good communication, forget grammar and pronunciation. Correcting the speaker just turns off the conversation. Make truly needed corrections at another time. You can say later, "By the way, the correct word is *lie*, not *lay*, in the sentence. . . ."

7. If you aren't knowledgeable on a topic, ask questions. Most young people love to be queried as an expert—it makes them feel more important.

8. Read and read more—not only topics you're interested in, but also subjects about the younger generation. Be familiar with pop musicians, professional athletes, the latest dances, and newest language terms—familiar enough so you can ask a question, get an answer, and thus learn more.

9. Avoid arguments and a combative attitude. Be willing to accept divergent points of view as part of your open nature. Be grand rather than grouchy.

10. Don't be the inquisitor. Sometimes it's best to gently switch subjects if you think you're pressing too hard and not getting anywhere.

11. Don't be judgmental. One grandparent asked a grandson what a certain drug was like, assuming he had had some experience with it. This judgmental question resulted in a judgmental response from the grandson: "I guess it's a lot like your use of alcohol, Grandpa." Carefully think through your method of introducing a touchy topic.

12. Avoid criticizing. It completely turns off the conversation. If you must pursue a subject such as your granddaughter's lavish use of makeup, ask a flat question (such as her favorite color of lipstick) and see where the conversation leads.

13. Avoid clichés, such as "My, you're a big boy" or "Have you been good?" or "What's up?" These are poor lead-ins to conversation, and sometimes kids are at a loss as to how to respond.

14. Don't pick on little things that don't really matter, such as hair styles, room neatness, clothing, or modern music. Think back about all the strange and weird things you did—and yet you turned out okay.

15. Don't overstep your bounds. If your grandchildren's parents are on the scene, don't say things like: "Isn't it time for the kids to go to bed?"

16. Don't correct your children in front of their children! You had your chance to parent, and it's too late to straighten out your kids. Unless they're doing something immoral or illegal, be quiet. If you have to speak your mind, talk with them in private. Don't erode the grandchildren's confidence in their parents.

17. Don't "talk down." Realize your grandchild's growing intelligence and vocabulary. Help a youngster to stretch her vocabulary.

18. Don't belittle what's important or of great concern in another's life. Kids today are much more aware of and involved in the challenges facing society. While they may not have solutions, this awareness should be nurtured.

19. Don't spell things out in the presence of little kids, such as "Mrs. Whitmore is p-r-e-g-n-a-n-t." It's rude. Besides, kids can spell, too. If it isn't to be discussed with kids, wait until they're out of sight and sound.

20. Speak facts, not generalities. Don't lump all kids, all music, all fashions together. After all, you wouldn't like generalities about fuddy-duddy old folks, would you?

21. Go easy on very personal topics. Wait until you know you are a confidante of that grandchild. Save these conversations for special one-on-one times.

22. Plant clues in your own conversation for others to pick up. If you say, "I was late because something appeared in my rose garden," perhaps someone will pick up the clue and ask you a question.

23. Regularly check the conversation for the level of boredom. If the participants are looking around as if they are hoping for a means of escape, it's time to quit talking and steer the conversation to another topic.

24. When going out for a visit or social function, always be prepared to talk on five topics, but see if you can get through an evening without using up your list. (This shows you were

thinking on the spot.) When you've mastered the five topics technique, share the idea with your grandkids.

25. No matter what, don't be offended by the words or deeds of your grandchildren. Forgive and forget the foolishness of youth and keep the door open for communication. That's the only way to maintain and improve your relationship.

Many parents in my survey indicated they wanted more input from their own parents and grandparents. So, *upon request,* be willing to share, to talk. Occasionally you may see the symptoms of a bad habit or serious problem cropping up in a grandchild. If you maintain good conversational links with your own child, the parent, you may be able to avert some behavioral disaster. After all, you've been through it and should have some wisdom and experience.

One of your best links to your grandchildren is conversation. Keep the lines open, and talk often.

GRANDPARENTS' WORKSHOP

If you're short on topics to talk about with your grandchildren, try asking these questions, which may be helpful in getting the conversation going:

For pre-school children:

* How does that train work?
* If you could have just one food to eat for a whole day, what would it be?
* What's your best friend like?
* How do you decide what to wear each day?
* What is the part of day you like best?
* What's your favorite character in a book?

Avoid: "My how you've grown!" "Do you like TV?" "Have you been good today?"

For grade-school youngsters:

* Are there any TV shows that remind you of your own life?
* If you could live in another country, which one would you choose?
* Would you ever want to be in the Olympics?
* What are the latest trends in school clothes, dress codes, and school uniforms?
* How many different nationalities are in your class? What have you learned from kids from other countries?
* What's the best thing that's happened to you this week?

Avoid: "What do you want to be when you grow up?" "Now when I was your age . . . " "Of course you like cauliflower."

For teens:

* Who are your present day heroes or role models?
* How has the women's liberation movement changed the rituals of dating?
* What emotions does your music evoke? (Note that you don't comment derogatorily on volume of music or appearance of performers.)
* What do you think you'll be doing in the year 2010?

* Are you a romantic or a realist? (You may be asked to define your terms, but at least that gets the conversation going!)
* When you have the money to buy a car, what kind do you think you'd like to drive?
* What's the hardest part of being on the team?
* What is your most prized possession?

Avoid: "When are you going to cut your hair?" "Are any of your friends pregnant?" "Why don't you improve your grades?"

Start talking! Start listening!

Two

THE SECOND COMMANDMENT:

You shall share your own unique talents with your grandchildren

Dear Grandma,

I don't know what's gotten into my son Michael! He's the father of two wonderful kids ages six and ten. These grandchildren are smart, but neither he nor his wife seems to have the good sense to teach them any skills or sports or even encourage their other talents. The kids spend most afternoons alone at home after school. They look at a lot of TV and seem bored. I don't like to butt in, but I feel their growing-up years are going by with nothing happening.

THE IMPATIENT GRANDMA

You're right. With grandchildren there are times to butt in and times to stay out. When it comes to enriching the lives of your grandchildren, this is the time to take an interest . . . but you must do it in the right way. Your son and daughter-in-law are probably not ignoring your grandchildren. They may be contributing ideas and spending time in many areas—areas you aren't aware of.

How wonderful that you want to have a positive impact on your grandchildren! This is far better than just being the old person who appears now and then to criticize and complain about everything. Some of your skills are ones you'll "teach" quite subtly. Others may take a more structured form. Either way, you'll be adding to your grandchildren's intelligence and making life better for them.

Start by considering just what talents you have to share. Also think about the time commitment you'd like to make and any possible cost involved. You may have a little extra money you can use or you may be on Social Security without a cent to spare—either way, you can have an impact. Your unique talents didn't disappear when you launched your own children. Now, you have the choice of sharing with another generation. And it *is* a choice.

When you have your ideas ready, talk about them with your son and daughter-in-law. Outline a simple plan and see how it fits in with their family life. Next, with the parents' blessing, approach your grandchildren with your ideas. Don't come on too strong with your ideas. Start small, but aim big.

Choose one skill or talent you know well and offer to share it. This might be car repairs, wood carving, tennis, sewing, baseball, painting, computer, or cooking. There are so many things a child should know, and a parent can't possibly cover them all.

Suggest a trial period of a month or two—long enough to see how well you work together. Then at the end of that time, assess the plan and refine it as necessary. Keep your list of things you feel comfortable sharing, but pursue just one at a time. Don't hesitate to switch to another idea if you feel the time and interest of the grandchild dictates a change. Most kids will be quite frank as to whether they're bored or intrigued with your ideas.

If you live close to grandchildren, your input will no doubt be on a regular basis. If you can spend only limited time with your grandchildren, you'll need to choose areas that can be covered more quickly or in a specified length of time. Above all, keep your sharing times happy and free of tension.

In my survey of grandparents, many different talents and topics were suggested. Here are some of the most popular:

1. Love of nature. Go on nature excursions to closely examine elements such as rocks, shells, leaves, or tide pools. Take along binoculars, a magnifying glass, and books that identify trees, birds, or flowers. You can either buy inexpensive books or borrow books from the library.

Teaching the names of stars and constellations is another aspect of nature, and it's fun to do it stretched out on a blanket at night. For daytime sky-viewing, teach the names of the various kinds of clouds.

2. How to drive. While many high schools provide good driving instruction classes, actual practice is important, and schools lack the time for it. So you can give some hands-on instruction. An unused large parking lot is a good place to start. Kids are eager to get behind the wheel and will appreciate your confidence in letting them practice. Share your time-proven safety tips, too.

Grandparents report that such driving practice sessions are great bonding experiences. And many young people say that a grandparent has lots more patience than a parent!

3. Cooking, baking. With fast foods and meals that come out of the microwave in just two minutes, many kids grow up not knowing how to cook. In general, home-made meals are much less expensive, so it's a real service to teach "cooking from scratch" to young people.

Start with toddlers, letting them take part in simple projects, such as making pudding or cookies. For older youngsters, continue with more elaborate dishes, showing them how to use the mixer, the food processor, and the blender.

Both boys and girls can benefit from your lessons in cooking. For especially interested children, buy a small recipe file and let them copy your prize recipes after you have made the dish together.

Cooking also provides good math lessons, especially when you double a recipe. Keeping safety in mind, let youngsters have as much hands-on experience as possible.

If you entertain, employ your grandchild to help you prepare the food, serve, and clean up. Such an arrangement is rewarding to both grandparent and grandchild.

4. Photography. One little girl reported to her grandfather that her dad said she couldn't take pictures because film was too expensive, and she wasted it by taking poor pictures. So the grandfather offered to give her a few photography lessons.

On his next visit, he brought along a basic camera and showed his granddaughter all the inner workings. He then provided a short roll of film, and together they embarked on an afternoon of photography. He gently explained picture composition, lighting, and focusing. When the first pictures came back, the two critiqued each one.

She was soon taking excellent pictures on her own—as even her dad agreed. In fact, he slightly increased her allowance to help pay for film and processing.

5. Reading. Books are among the greatest gifts from grandparent to grandchild. Often grandparents have the extra time to read "just one more story" or to listen patiently and encourage the struggling young reader.

Teach the love of reading by taking grandchildren to the library and occasionally the bookstore. Visit library book sales and used book stores. You'll be pleased with the bargains.

Show how to care for books and help a child establish a book shelf in his or her room. Don't keep reading the same stories; find others by the same author. And introduce new authors.

See if a child can tell the story by looking only at the pictures. Then make up a new story by looking at the pictures. Let reading be fun! Encourage a child to read at least thirty minutes each day.

Many reading games, plus a list of "best-ever" books, can be found in my book *1001 Things to Do with Your Kids* (Abingdon Press, 1988).

6. Workshop. Woodcraft, power tool use, home repair—these are talents that have gotten lost in the era of easy and cheap replacements and throw-away items. However, the competence and patience required in working with one's hands are invaluable skills still taught by wise grandfathers, and some wise grandmothers, too.

But safety comes first with a serious approach to the use of tools. Teach respect for tools and patiently oversee the practice sessions until the child gains confidence. As one little boy put it: "Grandpa showed me how to carve wood without carving my fingers."

A smart grandmother found that tools fit nicely into Christmas stockings, so she buys one for each grandchild yearly. These gifts are part of the child's growing tool kit and provide the incentive to get tool-friendly before leaving the nest.

One grandfather invites a grandson over for a weekly workshop session, starting in the summer, to help the youngster make Christmas gifts for his family and friends. Treasure boxes, trivets, small bookshelves, bookends, and doorstops are some of his accomplishments.

7. Computer. If there is a computer at the grandparents' house, there's no need to worry about grandchildren being bored. Learning new computer skills and games can provide worthwhile activity on a rainy day when inside activities are needed.

One grandfather even does the rotation schedule for his granddaughter's soccer team. But she has to help him do it. This gives him an important link to her, since he's invited to the games and the final dinner for being part of the adult support group.

8. Sewing, knitting. These money-saving skills used to be for girls only, but now boys are learning them and are not ashamed of it. One grandmother helped a grandson design and knit a big bulky sweater he proudly wears to school.

The same grandmother made a "contract" with her grand-daughter. In return for a pledge of no smoking/no drinking/no drug use, the grandmother promised to provide the fabric and guidance for making a new article of clothing every month. Together, they pick out the pattern and material. Then, at the grandmother's home, they evenly divide the work and complete the project.

Sometimes the grandmother surprises the granddaughter by doing the finishing work of buttons and buttonholes and trim. But the granddaughter is getting proficient at that, too. One big project was a fabulous prom dress—one that the teen never could have afforded to buy ready-made.

9. Painting. While young children are encouraged to paint at school and home, older ones with some talent lack opportunities to learn real skills. Many grandparents proficient in water color, oil painting, and collage are providing this teaching, plus "studios" for practice at their own home.

One grandmother reports that she and her nine-year-old twin grandchildren have a weekly session with three easels for the three artists working together. She reports that they enjoy talking and painting at the same time.

Another grandmother says that her grandson is earning a living in art—a subject he knew little of until she introduced him to ceramics when he was in high school.

Art equipment is expensive: paints, easels, a kiln, a potter's wheel, and so forth. But many of these things may already exist at the grandparent's home.

One grandmother combines art and nature by taking her granddaughter to scenic places where they paint together for a few hours each week. The grandmother picks the girl up after school and brings her home about the time her working mother gets home.

10. Athletics. Sports proficiency is one of the most important areas for grandparent aid. Beyond simple throwing and catching, grandparents can teach batting, skiing, skating, fishing, horseback riding, tennis, golf, and swimming, sailing, and other water sports. Most of these provide excellent opportunities for building memories together.

Several sports are time-consuming, as well as money-consuming. Sometimes a grandparent is able to provide equipment and also pay sports fees. But some parents are happy to pay the bills in return for the grandparent's input of time and talent.

A grandfather who presented his extra set of golf clubs to a grandson, and also taught him the basics of the game, was rewarded some years later. When the elderly grandfather could no longer drive his own car, the grandson was glad to pick him up and drive to the golf course. Once there, the young man was a proficient part of the twosome, but the grandfather insisted on paying the green fees. It was a good deal for both of them.

11. The love of poetry. This is a rather unusual talent one of my survey grandparents shares, but worth mentioning since it shows the broad range of possibilities.

This grandmother really loves poetry. She lives far from her grandchildren, so she often writes to them in verse. When she buys books for them, they are rhyme or poetry books. She records herself reading poetry. She sends these cassettes to them as bedtime listening. And when they visit her, she reads poetry aloud to them.

She always has a poetry book on the dining table and insists that the reading of poetry while eating improves digestion. Over the phone or by mail, she gives the youngsters suggestions for writing poetry. And once a year she has a poetry writing contest for all her grandchildren with prizes for every participant. While she doesn't know if she's encouraged the great poet of the twenty-first century, she has certainly interested these young people in the written and rhymed word.

Some of the above skills and interests can be shared on grandparent/grandchild visits or vacations, or on monthly or even yearly get-togethers.

For grandparents who see grandchildren weekly, there are even greater opportunities.

With the parent's permission, be willing to take over an entire area of your grandchild's education. This is a major commitment of time, talent, and perhaps even money, but is a lifelong gift to a grandchild. Here are some examples:

1. Tutoring. If a child is doing poorly in a school subject, see if you can help. Spelling, math, reading—these basic skills are vitally important to a child's success in life. If your help can make a difference, certainly offer your time.

You will want to talk this over with both the child and parent present, so there is no misunderstanding as to your input. Be specific as to what you will be doing, also where, when, and how often. It may even be possible for you to be in touch with the teacher to ascertain specific problems and progress.

One grandmother, a librarian, has taught each of her grandchildren the skill of doing research and reference work—a skill that put them ahead in both high school and college classes.

2. Educational enrichment. After-school reading classes, French or other language lessons, art, speech, and computer classes are usually held on a weekly basis. As a grandparent, you can provide as much as you choose in support of these classes: a ride there and back, payment of class fees, homework help, and practice time at your house.

And there are opportunities for *you* to learn right along with your grandchild. Many grandparents go back to school for classes offered at junior colleges, through a university extension, or at special summer sessions. Everything from magic to mountain climbing is taught. You can even do your homework with your grandchild.

3. Music and dance lessons. Weekly lessons that go on for several years can be a major expenditure for a family. If you are interested in helping, decide in advance of your offer just how much you want to be involved.

Do you want to pay for some part of the lessons? Perhaps you can make the ballerina's costume, or pay the rental on the trumpet. Or, you may be a big spender and want to give the family a piano!

But if your budget is much smaller, you can still help. Are you able to take the child to and from the lesson? Would you enjoy supervising some of the practice times? (Parents find that getting kids to practice is often a hassle and would love to have someone help with this.) One of the nicest forms of support is to go to the recital, play, or concert, and applaud the efforts of a grandchild. No one can have too many boosters.

4. Religious training. Today's busy parents often fail to see the importance of weekly religious observances. Going to church or temple is just one more "must do" in an already hectic week.

Many grandparents who are regular church attenders find that it is easy to take on this aspect of a grandchild's education. Driving them to religious classes or Sunday school (and perhaps having brunch afterwards) can be a successful project for the present with lifelong rewards. One grandfather reports that his grandchildren talked so much about the good times they had together that the parents began attending church, too.

In my survey of grandparents, I was impressed by the great number who emphasized religion as one of the foremost subjects to teach a grandchild. These grandparents spoke of helping grandchildren love the Bible and other religious books, of teaching them how to pray about daily challenges, and of sharing the comfort of God's love for all God's children.

Certainly a firm conviction in a caring God is a benefit for any child. But children of broken families, as well as children who have been neglected or abused by parents, find special comfort in relying on their own heavenly Parent for guidance and love.

5. Values. Society's disregard for values has upset many grandparents. Many of those I interviewed said they are their grandchildren's sole teachers of ethics and morals. While that may not be quite true, it is important for children to have many good role models.

These subjects are not ones that can be taught like piano lessons. But, in many ways, good character traits are more important to success than some forms of educational training.

Grandparents specifically mentioned their role teaching in these six areas:

* Independence
* Honesty
* Patriotism
* Orderliness and having a system
* Kindness and tolerance of others
* Good manners

Some of these ideals were taught through one-on-one conversations and some were taught only by example.

A grandfather said he would donate a flag to his grandchildren's home if they were willing to learn flag history and flag etiquette. They got so involved in talking about the U.S. war for independence, the personal price of patriotism, and the evolution of our flag, that a weekend project went on for several months. What started as a plan to install a wall-mounted pole by the front door turned into a project that included a much bigger pole set in cement in the ground. Eventually a light on a timer was set up to shine on the flag.

Responsibility was also tackled by grandparents. One grandmother helped a teen work out a system to get his sports and other activities in balance with his homework. Another helped a granddaughter reorganize her closet, desk, and chest of drawers for greater efficiency.

A most charming idea came from a grandmother who prepared the after-school snack as if it were a party. Her grandchildren stopped by weekly for her special event, and they even brought friends. One granddaughter said it was like a fancy finishing school. The grandmother suggested good manners in eating, how to make conversation, and ways of being appreciative. And she taught her two grandchildren to write thank-you notes—something she says they still did well ten years later.

"Who shall we be kind to this week?" was a question posed each Friday by a grandmother to her grade-school grandson. Sometimes he suggested a sick pal, a neighbor, a teacher, or sometimes himself. The pair would then set about to make some cookies or other treat, and also a cheery card for that person. It didn't take more than an hour or so before they were ready to make their "Kindness Delivery." Then the grandson was driven home, feeling happy and satisfied with his part in this caring project.

6. Season tickets. Buying a series of tickets is an automatic way to spend time together. Of course you'll want to have a good talk with your grandchild before subscribing to a series. The youngster needs to feel a commitment or willingness to take part. The time spent in getting to the event and home again is great for conversation, and the event itself can be fun, as well as a satisfying learning experience.

Some series to consider are: youth plays, baseball or football games, community concerts, or summer theater.

7. School contact. Working parents often find it impossible to attend many school functions, including important PTA meetings, sports events, class days, teacher-parent interviews, and events needing chaperons.

Schools welcome the participation of grandparents in many of these areas. While room-*mothers* used to be a popular volunteer job for a parent, many schools are eager for room-*grandmothers* nowadays. One teacher said, "Grandmothers are more patient and they seem to enjoy going on the school fieldtrips more than mothers and fathers." It may have been some time since you helped a group of kids tour a museum or dairy farm, but you will probably get a kick out of it.

Having grandparents who attend events such as parent's night, school pancake breakfasts, and plays can add to a child's self-esteem. "Someone cares about you" is what you're saying. And a grandparent can help keep a busy parent informed about the school's activities.

The most important school event is usually the every-semester parent-teacher conference. Often these are held in the hour after the school day ends—a time inconvenient for working parents. But a grandparent could take this on, listening, talking, and making good notes for sharing with parent and child later.

8. Leading a group. There is always a shortage of leaders for youth groups such as Scouts, Indian Guides, Camp Fire, and Boys and Girls Clubs. While these jobs used to be the prerogative (and duty) of parents, today many others are helping out. Childless business people and grandparents are finding this activity a good investment in the future success of our youth.

You would probably be making a one-year commitment, plus time for some training, weekly meetings, and special trips and events. This leadership position is definitely worth considering since you'll be contributing your talents to a larger number of children, rather than to just your own grandchild. Such unselfishness is rewarded in many surprising ways. One grandfather saved over seven hundred dollars in auto repairs when his senior scout group volunteered to redo his transmission.

As you teach your grandchild the many useful things she can do, it is sometimes helpful to provide a place to gather these facts. Here's one way to do it.

When each grandchild learns to read, buy a little file box for him to keep. With a label machine, make a title for the box, such as "Cary's Messages from Grandma and Grandpa." Put dividers into the box for many categories, such as hobbies, repairs, cooking, family history, sayings, automotive, poems, and places to go.

When you answer a grandchild's question, or when you teach him something, put the important information on a three-by-five-inch card for the box. These cards can tell how to make a meatloaf, what kind of oil goes in the car, foods you especially like, your favorite brand of cologne or after-shave, how to sew on a button so it won't come off, birth dates of family members, names and addresses of relatives, the best kinds of glue for various uses, how long to fire a ceramic piece, your favorite punch ingredients, a list of local excursions you'd like to make together, or little messages of love and encouragement.

Add to the box on every visit—and by mail. As you become a specialist for your grandchild, let him become a specialist on you.

GRANDPARENTS' WORKSHOP

Make a three-generation quilt.

Many hands and many skills are involved in this interesting project. Remember that this is NOT a grandma project, but one that can use help from grandpa and all the grandchildren.

Follow these steps:

1. Write to all the family members—cousins, uncles, aunts, parents, and grandparents. Ask them to trace around their outstretched right hand on a piece of paper. Also ask them for a piece of material that they like. This can be in a favorite color or pattern, even a piece of cloth from something they no longer use or wear. You many want to include a stamped return envelope to encourage the return of these hand tracings and fabrics.

2. While waiting for the hands to come back, buy a large quilt or comforter in a solid color. You also can start from scratch and make a comforter (if you choose to do it the hard way).

3. Trace the paper hands onto the pieces of fabric using carbon paper. Then carefully cut out the hands. Be sure to put a temporary paper label on each piece of fabric so you know whose hand it is.

4. Using straight pins, affix the hands to the quilt (palms in the center, fingers pointing outward). Put them in a large circle or oval, depending on the size of the quilt and the number of hands. Vary the sizes of hands—small, medium, large. See that the thumb of one hand touches the little finger of the next hand.

5. You may want to put some batting behind each hand to plump it up before using thread to tack it in place.

6. Appliqué each hand into place, using colored thread. Two or more can work on this at the same time.

7. Above the fingertips of each hand, stitch or embroider the first name of the appropriate family member. These names form an outer circle around the circle of hands.

8. Finally, let all who helped construct the quilt stitch their names on the back side. Also stitch the date the quilt was completed.

This quilt makes a wonderful family remembrance, a great wall hanging, or a gift for a special anniversary or birthday.

Three

THE THIRD COMMANDMENT:

You shall explore the wonders of the past with your grandchildren

Dear Grandma,

We consider ourselves modern grandparents. We certainly don't live in the past, but we'd like our grandchildren to appreciate their heritage and know some of the things that happened long before they were born. Do you agree that this could be helpful to them?

VETERAN GRANDPA

I certainly do! The following excerpt from "The Chapel of the Hermits" by John Greenleaf Whittier says it well:

For all of good the past hath had
Remains to make our own time glad.

In order to have those glad times the poem mentions, you must find a way to share the good of the past. You can't keep the past to yourself. What happened in days gone by can be a guide to the present and enliven the future.

Grandparents should neither feel hesitant about talking about past history, nor should they withhold the enrichment gained through years of living. In sharing, they should include the challenges and defeats of previous generations right along with the wondrous achievements. Most kids are fascinated to know what life was like in wartime, in another part of the world, or before the wonders of cable TV, FAX machines, computers, superhighways, supersonic jets, and two-minute dinners.

The question is how to present the past to grandchildren in an interesting way. It doesn't need to sound like a boring history lecture. The grandparents in my survey spoke enthusiastically about ways to bring the past into the present with family reunions, trips back to old neighborhoods, and even making a family tree.

It's disheartening to note, though, that 16 percent of the grandparents said they did absolutely nothing to share family heritage. Some felt that talking about the past just wasn't worthwhile. One grandfather said he wasn't proud of his background because he had an ancestor who was a European gangster. Now I think that story is definitely worth sharing!

Sometimes communicating information about our past—even information that might not make us proud—helps us to recognize all the progress we have made. Also, stories of challenges show the human struggle—a struggle that can eventually end in triumph. I say, don't hold back those stories, no matter how wild they are.

Grandparents who participated in my survey also described simple ideas that could be shared on a day-to-day basis or when making a long visit from afar. Let's start with the most commonly recommended way of making the link to the past.

Photographs—Past and Present

Attention! Do not sit down with your grandchild and go through all the family photo albums in one afternoon. Just a few at a time has a greater effect. A few pages on each visit is plenty. Kids love to see photos that show their parents as children, that show old-fashioned cars and houses, or that show how life was lived a generation or more ago. But, they can't absorb it all in one sitting.

Take a photo album when you go to visit. Have one ready to share when the grandchildren visit you. Use a bright ribbon to mark the place in the album where you stopped, so you'll know where to pick up the next time.

The "who's who" in photos is important. If you haven't done so already, go through your photos and make identification captions telling who the people are and where and when the picture was taken. Resolve to do this with all the new photos you take. We think we will always remember, but. . . .

Don't hesitate to take a photo out of the album. (See chapter 11 for the photo on the dining table.) Put some photos in frames, on tables, or on the wall. Or tape a couple of photos on a mirror. Change them before a grandchild visits. You'll like the variety, too.

If you have two fairly similar photos and you can spare one, give it to your grandchild for her family photo album.

Your Grandchild's Photo Album

Start a photo album for each grandchild. At the beginning, include some pictures of ancestors. Then include pictures of yourself, followed by yourself with your children—the grandchild's parent. Ask the parents for some early photos of your grandchild. Taking the time to prepare photo albums is not a high priority for today's busy parents. Their photos may be heaped in an old shoe box so you'll be doing them a favor by getting at least a few of them into an album.

Add to the album by giving the youngster newer pictures as you take them. If you live far away, these pictures will keep the grandchildren up-to-date on your activities. Also, they are a helpful reminder of what you look like. If you're nearby, the pictures can include you and your grandchild. If you have several grandchildren, this is where those double print offers come in handy.

Keep up this photo sharing tradition through the years. Soon you'll find your grandchild sharing photos with you.

Storytelling

The next step beyond the photo album is to tell stories about the people in the pictures. According to my survey of grandparents, storytelling was the second most favorite method of sharing history. One grandmother said, "Having to tell a story about people in the photographs made me remember so many fascinating and funny things that happened when I was young. I enjoyed it as much as my grandson!"

Let your storytelling be very specific. Get out a map or globe if necessary. Tell where and when these people lived. Why are they wearing odd clothes? What did they do all day without TV? Was this person an artist? A farmer? A coal miner? A legislator? A women's rights activist? A World War I soldier? Don't tell just the happy endings; share the tragedies, too. The sad occasions make the happy times more meaningful.

One grandmother names each story that she tells. Some of her titles are "The Legend of the Lost Brother," "Who Wants to Live in Minnesota?" and "Why Sparkie the Dog Got His Picture Taken."

Children of grade-school age and up are often interested in love stories. How grandpa found grandma and how they fell in love and got married can be a marvelous example to young people. And everyone loves a wedding. Share your wedding photo album, too.

Always popular among grandchildren are stories about their parents as kids—this gives a whole new perspective to mom and dad. They actually did crazy things? Mom got dirty making mud-pies? Dad had shoulder-length hair? They took pictures kissing in a automatic photo booth? Kids wonder if these can be the same folks they know today.

Stories told with photos are great at bedtime. You don't have to be right on hand at the bedside, either. One grandfather occasionally calls at bedtime to tell an intriguing story over the phone. Sometimes he sends a photo in advance—a photo with no identification. This interests the grandchildren and they can't wait for the telephone tale.

One young grandchild commented on a grandfather's story about a war he had served in: "Wow, he remembers old wars, so maybe he knew George Washington, or even Moses!"

The Written Word

If you have legible handwriting or a typewriter or word processor, consider writing a family history. This won't be done in a day, but it is a worthwhile long-term project, and your children and grandchildren can help. When the history is completed, have a family get-together where each member is given his or her own copy. Putting each in a sturdy loose-leaf binder helps preserve the copies for the future. Such histories also make great nostalgic gifts for anniversaries or birthdays.

A family history should include full given names, maiden names and surnames, and birth dates or years when available. The earliest recalled relatives and their country of origin should be listed. A complete history would include stories that have been handed down about them. Try to include their dates of immigration, occupations, talents, hobbies, marriage dates, and number of children. Where possible, include the names of all children—a rich source of names for new babies that will be added to the family. Also, if there are pictures or furnishings that once belonged to those ancestors and are still being used in the family, note that, too. The person compiling the history and the compilation date should be included as well.

It's especially helpful if one family member takes on the job of making a yearly update of this family history. This chronicle of the past year should include new births, graduations, weddings, deaths, job changes, homes bought, trips taken, and so forth. A copy should be made of the yearly update and sent to each family member to add to his family history book.

One artistic grandparent put copies of the family history into sturdy file folders and labeled them "My Heritage Book." She decorated each one and also put the grandchild's name on the cover.

There also are heritage books that you can buy and fill in. They include places for dates and photos. But the home-made kind is still the best.

The Family Tree

In a heritage book, it helps keep everyone straight if you include a family tree. Instructions on how to do this are at the end of this chapter in the "Grandparents' Workshop" section.

Sometimes it's educational to display a big family tree on the wall near the dining table, or in the family room. You may want to make a large one on art paper or shelf paper and pass it from family to family every few months, or take it along when you go to visit relatives.

A family tree is especially helpful when you're going to have a large get-together with many relatives.

Seeing just how everyone is related is useful to grandchildren—and many of the older folks, too.

Cassette Messages

For far-away relatives, here's one of the best and most personal ways to share history. Cassette tapes let grandparents tell stories and share news. This way the grandchildren can hear the grandparents' voices. While some grandparents read story books from the library onto the cassette, many others enjoy recording stories from events in the past. These are helpful when a parent is too busy to tell bedtime stories.

An oral history can also be compiled on cassette with various relatives telling stories of early family history. It's especially meaningful to the family to have these recordings after the storyteller has passed on. Try to get these tales in chronological order. It helps if one person narrates the cassette, serving as a link by introducing each speaker and telling that person's relationship in the family.

Videos

It's very hard for grandchildren to remember all the distant relatives. One set of grandparents settled this problem by making a video cassette. They introduced themselves and showed some of the things they did in a typical day: leaving for work, walking the dog, playing croquet.

They also filmed a walking tour through their house and yard. The video included specific places of interest to grandchildren who were to visit that summer: the guest bedroom, the family room, the swing on the front porch, the store where they shopped, the local movie house, and the park.

The last part of the video showed neighbors, friends, and other relatives who lived nearby giving words of welcome to the grandchildren and telling how much they were looking forward to meeting the grandchildren.

Along with the video they sent a local map with stars showing the location of grandma and grandpa's house, a cousin's home, shops, church, the park and zoo, and even the ice cream store.

This video was a real hit with the grandchildren, who played it many times and even asked their friends over to watch it. When they made their summer visit they felt right at home, having "been there" before via the video.

Ethnic History

Don't fail to give grandchildren an understanding of and appreciation for their ethnic background. Yes, the world is becoming a melting-pot society, but the individual ingredients in the melting pot still have vitality and value. With borders and governments changing rapidly around the world, this ethnic education is both a history and a geography lesson for young people.

Expose grandchildren to ethnic foods. Share old family recipes. Tell stories of eating spanakopita, smorgasbord, or spetzle when you were young. Keep the traditions alive by serving some cultural dishes and celebrating ethnic holidays.

Hunt through your musical recordings and find some music typical of your family's native country. Play these for your grandchildren and explain special musical instruments. Perhaps you can even demonstrate ethnic dances such as the Highland Fling, the hula, or the Russian Cossack dance.

Some cities have ethnic festivals, parades, and concerts. Take your grandchildren to these events. These can increase appreciation for different family heritages and so they actually decrease feelings of racism or bigotry. Emphasize both the uniqueness and the equality of each culture.

A Visit to the "Old Neighborhood"

In the place you were raised, and also the one where you raised your children, history and memories still reside, even if the "old neighborhood" has changed.

When it is convenient, take your grandchildren back to these neighborhoods. Let them see the houses. Perhaps you'll be bold enough to ring the doorbell and ask if you can take a peek! If you know, show them where your parents (their great-grandparents) were born or raised.

Visit schools, parks, and shops that you knew in earlier years. Consider lunching at your former favorite restaurant or deli. Walk the streets and get a feeling for another era, exploring this with the grandchildren. Compare the old with the new and talk about the differences.

With proper advance conversation to alleviate any sadness, make a visit to the cemetery to see old family gravestones. This can be educational and not depressing. If you do this near Memorial Day (or any time of the year), let the grandchildren take part in the old tradition of placing flowers on the graves of ancestors.

When going on such nostalgia trips, it's a good idea to take along the family tree so that youngsters can keep track of "who's who" when you're talking about relatives they've never met. Such trips give kids added appreciation for their roots.

Reunions

These big events can be intimidating or invigorating, depending on how well they are planned and executed. Sometimes there is a mini-reunion at a wedding, birthday, or funeral. But the best reunions take place when the get-together itself is the focal point.

A reunion needs to include the right mix of unstructured time for talk and structured time for joyful activities. Announce the reunion date well in advance and keep reminding relatives of how special it would be to have them attend.

Spread the work and encourage attendance by giving everyone an assignment (certain games, activities, foods, stories). Participation also makes kids better behaved. And it puts shy folks at ease.

Here are some tried and true ideas:

1. Greeters. Teens do a great job of parking cars, carrying luggage and food, watching babies, and in general making everyone feel at home. Use name tags if it's a big crowd where some don't know all the others. Give each person a list of those attending with addresses and telephone numbers, and a copy of the official family tree so each one can see how she fits into the big family picture.

2. Video camera interviews. As relatives arrive, videotape their entrance and first comments. Have an older teen or adult running the camera, another asking questions. Each one interviewed should be asked his name and where he came from, along with his relationship to the family. These are fun to view after the reunion and can also be played at the next reunion.

3. Food. Somehow this is always the highlight! Make the first meal a real potluck since those traveling can bring cookies, rolls, jams, and other foods that travel well. Provide cards on the buffet table so that each dish is identified: "Uncle Jim's pickle relish," "Cousin Sandy's lemon pie."

4. The Photo. While many pictures will be taken, be sure to set aside one time when the entire group is photographed. Use a professional photographer or the very best picture-taker in the family—providing there's a remote control so the *photographer* can get into the picture, too. Choose a well-lighted place, with perhaps something historical in the background (the old farm house, huckleberry hill, or the village square monument). This photo will become a permanent family record and and will be looked at time and time again, so everyone should be dressed nicely and have pleasant expressions—no horseplay or fingers behind heads for this one!

Copies of it (eight-by-ten-inch or bigger and suitable for hanging) will probably be in demand. Provide a sign-up list and a money jar so that those who want one can contribute a set sum. When the copies are on hand and ready to be mailed, provide a row-by-row, left-to-right identification caption with each picture.

5. Recognition. There should be a designated-in-advance master of ceremonies who gets everyone's attention at the main event and does the job of official welcoming. Certain people should definitely be recognized: the relative who traveled the greatest distance, the oldest and youngest attending, those attending for the first time, kids who have graduated or received other special honors, newlyweds, the family with the most children, the person with the best sunhat, and some other humorous distinctions.

6. Events. Depending on the location, you'll want some games, relays, and athletic events. A baseball game and swimming are "musts" in the summertime. A snowball fight between the generations and sledding are good winter activities. For games and relay races, see that every able-bodied relative is on a team. You may also want to have team cheerleaders. Favorites are tug-of-war, three-legged race, watermelon-eating contest, and the egg-catching contest.

7. Singing. If your invitation encourages the bringing of instruments and music, this will enhance the time set aside for singing. In the evening, around the outdoor fire or the indoor fireplace, let oldsters and youngsters request additional solos or group songs. For three-generation singing, you may want to make up some song sheets. The following songs are some of the most popular to include: "Shine on Harvest Moon," "I've Been Working on the Railroad," "Yellow Submarine," "O What a Beautiful Morning," "Row Your Boat," "For Me and My Gal," "On the Sunny Side of the Street," "Raindrops Keep Fallin' on My Head," "I'm Forever Blowing Bubbles," and "Seventy-six Trombones."

8. Pancake Breakfast. Even in this liberated society, much of the cooking will have been done by women. Let the men take over the final pancake breakfast. Provide aprons and chef's hats for the cooks, and a variety of pancake toppings for the pancake eaters.

9. Next date. Try to announce the date of the next reunion while spirits are high. Even get some volunteers to start plans.

Some other ideas are: a progressive supper with appetizer, main dish, salad, and dessert served at different homes; a small band for dancing; square dancing to recorded music; a cookie bake-off the last day so that everyone has cookies for the trip home.

Although most reunions are held at one family's home on a single weekend, some families hold them at a resort or campground and turn them into a short vacation.

Wherever it's held, the local relatives will of necessity have done much of the event planning and food preparation, so it's only fair if the location is different the next time.

How often? Some families have a yearly reunion. But most find that every three to five years is frequent enough. In that time span, the family has changed sufficiently to make the event very fascinating, and the space between is not so great that people forget each other or the joy of being together.

If your family hasn't had a family reunion recently, start planning one for the future—you'll want to do it again! This is history in the making.

GRANDPARENTS' WORKSHOP

Making a family tree for a grandchild

The tree you make will be slightly different for each family of grandchildren you have. But the basic structure will be the same.

Start by collecting the complete names of all relatives as far back as you can remember or research. If you can, also find dates of births, marriages, and deaths.

You probably will want to copy this basic tree form onto a much larger piece of paper.

Begin at the bottom by filling in the names of the grandchildren in one family. Then work up the family tree to the oldest-known relatives.

Be sure to include second marriages by listing the second name directly under the first.

Show uncles, aunts, and cousins, too.

If you are working on a very large piece of paper, you'll have space to include small photos of each person.

With patient and careful attention to all the details, this family tree will become an heirloom and a great discussion starter.

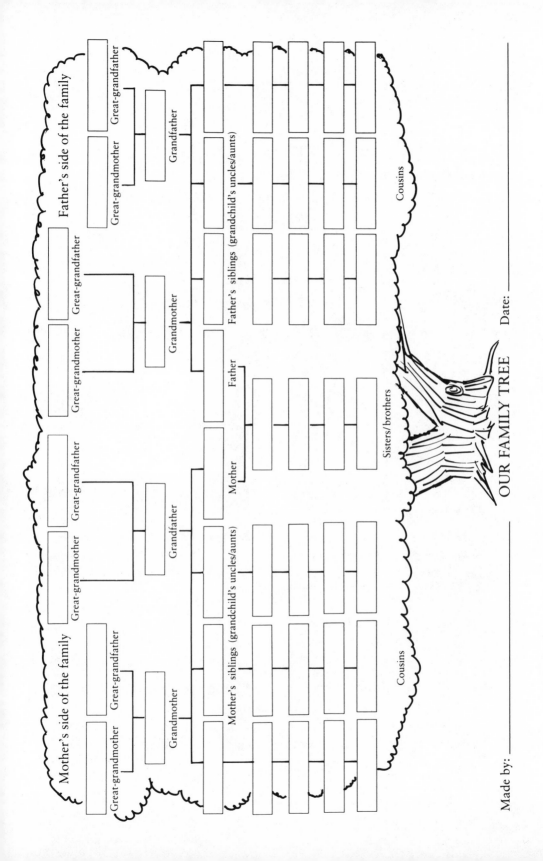

Mother's side of the family

Great-grandmother
Great-grandfather
Great-grandmother
Great-grandfather
Great-grandmother
Great-grandfather
Great-grandmother
Great-grandfather

Grandmother
Grandfather

Mother

Mother's siblings (grandchild's uncles/aunts)

Cousins

Father's side of the family

Great-grandfather
Great-grandmother
Great-grandmother
Great-grandfather

Grandmother
Grandfather

Father

Father's siblings (grandchild's uncles/aunts)

Sisters/brothers

Cousins

OUR FAMILY TREE   Date: _____

Made by: _____

Four

THE FOURTH COMMANDMENT:

You shall open your house and heart to your grandchildren

Dear Grandma,

Was I ever shocked today when I told our teenager Emily we were having dinner at Grandma's on Sunday and she said, "Oh Mom, do I have to go?" Our younger son Matt added, "Yeah, it's boring!" We live in the same town with my husband's parents, so what do we do about this problem?

WORRIED MOM

Give the grandparents a copy of this book! You will want them to read this chapter in particular, and then be very supportive of the new ideas your in-laws will be using.

Grandparents: Make your house a very comfortable second home for your grandchildren, but let it be quite different from their own home. Here, under your roof, life is more leisurely and low key. There aren't as many things that *must* be done. When visiting you, your own children usually make fewer demands on their kids, so everyone should be able to relax and enjoy the time together.

At grandma and grandpa's house, life should be more like a child's best dream. Different people are in charge and different rules apply. Surprises, appreciation, and hugs punctuate the time together. Conversation is unhurried and everyone gets to be heard. Meals are leisurely with laughing and storytelling. Spur-of-the-moment activities take place. Playtime isn't quickly terminated; most every activity can be "played out" to a satisfying end. Clocks don't rule. To-do lists are forgotten. This is an oasis in the busy desert of modern living.

If this does not describe life at your home, perhaps there are some changes you can make, changes that will make your grandchildren happy to visit, and changes that will make you eager to have them come.

An Environment for Children

While I believe that toddlers should be taught to respect the possessions of others, and in some cases to just look and not touch, you'll feel more at ease if priceless irreplaceables are put safely in a closet or out of reach when the little ones are on hand.

In their own home, your grandchildren should be given strict rules about climbing on furniture, taking things that don't belong to them, where to snack and eat, and what places are off-limits. (Yes, parents are entitled to areas in their own home that are restful, unstained, and toy-free.) While this necessary training will carry over to your home, the transfer of good behavior sometimes takes a while. So make a few modifications for peace of mind.

When crawlers and toddlers are visiting, you'll want to child-proof your home. This means you'll be alert to lamp cords, unused electric outlets, and the safe storage of cleaning supplies, medicines, knives, chemicals, and other harmful items. Stairways and swimming pools may require added protection.

As the kids get older, be prepared for curiosity. When grandchildren feel comfortable at your house, they are apt to pick up and read your mail or magazines, use your power tools, and eat crumby chocolate cookies on your pale pink upholstery. Gently establish what items and areas are out-of-bounds at your house.

Equipped for Action

Once the house is child safe, take inventory of what you have to make the visit fun. There are many simple supplies you can keep on hand. The toys you have are special, since they are not played with as often.

Don't rush to bring the toys and games out the minute grandkids come in the door. First talk about and take an interest in what *they've* brought to play with or share. Let the grandchildren take the lead; don't appear to be in a rush to get them organized and out of the way.

Of course, grandparenting "equipment" will vary with the age of the grandchildren, but here are some inexpensive kid-approved items to keep in a closet for those times when the grandkids need something to do:

For Pre-schoolers:
1. Clay (get the least expensive kind).
2. Plastic containers (like margarine dishes) and spoons for play outside or inside.
3. Building blocks (try a lumber yard for scrap wood that you can sand).
4. Dolls, stuffed animals, and packing boxes (houses) for imaginative play.
5. A wagon or trike.
6. Finger paints, aprons, and inexpensive paper.
7. Hand puppets.
8. Simple rolling toys.

For Gradeschoolers:
1. Kites.
2. Inexpensive airplane kits.

3. Monopoly, checkers, and box games.
4. Lego or other construction kits.
5. Non-violent action toys and converters.
6. Easel and paints.
7. Paper cut-outs.
8. Race cars.

For Teens
1. Trivia games.
2. Horseshoes.
3. Skateboard.
4. Puzzles.
5. Magic tricks.
6. Card games.

Also keep on hand a supply of books and records appropriate for the ages of the youngsters.

When you know grandchildren are coming, clear a table for games. Have an inexpensive dropcloth for young artists to work on. Provide a cardtable and a sheet for making a playhouse. Get ready for action!

Dinner at Grandma and Grandpa's

The most common three-generation get-together is the weekend meal. Why do we have to tie everything into eating? Perhaps, realizing we have to have a meal, we think: "I can do it best." And our busy children may be thinking, "Let someone other than us do the cooking." But the real reason is tradition—our parents did it, so we do it. Sitting around a table was comfortable and conversational. And it still can be.

The problem is that it often becomes just a routine. The seating arrangement is always the same. The cursory conversation is the same. The admonition to use good manners is the same. Even the menu is often the same! (See the Grandparents' Workshop at the end of this chapter for some easy-to-make menu suggestions.) As good as the food is, a lifetime of routine meals can dampen any good relationship.

While parents may be pleased to have someone else in charge of feeding the troops, this is often the kids' dreaded meal. The adults talk to one another, ignoring the kids except to correct or discipline them. It's not exactly a forum for fun.

Here are some ideas for making it an anticipated event:

1. Include all three generations in the table talk. A spirited conversation including everyone around the table can make any meal a great success, but this doesn't happen automatically and someone (you!) may have to be the guide to better conversation. Encourage everyone to bring a topic (camping experiences, birthday parties, pets, first jobs, sports, weddings, teachers, world peace, the comics, jokes, trips, or gardens). In advance of the meal, you'll want to tell your grandchild one of the topics *you* plan to bring up so she can think of something to contribute at the table. Be especially sensitive, patient, and encouraging to the conversational attempts of younger children. Listen attentively. Ask questions.

Don't rush from topic to topic. Stay with one until everyone has had a say. Just because you've finished dessert, you don't have to get up and leave. Some of the best conversations take place around the table when the meal is over and the diners are feeling mellow and well-fed.

2. Encourage a more casual meal. Dishes such as cheese fondue with everyone dipping bread into the pot, or make-your-own sundaes, encourage camaraderie and conversation. Let everyone participate in meal preparation, serving, and clean-up. Sometimes grandmas want to do it all, but don't be the little red hen! If you must keep control of the main course, let others prepare an appetizer, salad, or dessert. Perhaps one grandchild can bicycle over to your house an hour ahead and be a helper. Working together is fun and can be a bonding experience.

3. Use alternative places to eat. Try eating on the patio or in the yard (great when children are small and still spill food), around the fireplace, or in the park. Picnics are a pleasant change of pace and give kids freedom for play if the parents and grandparents want to talk a long while. One large family living in a warm climate has Thanksgiving dinner in the park each year, a tradition they heartily recommend.

4. Include special touches that give uniqueness to the meal. Let a grandchild make place cards or place mats. Let her serve an appetizer, perhaps one she's made. With a grandchild's help as a waiter, pretend it is a restaurant and prepare a menu. Have a few choices on your menu: salad dressing, vegetable, beverage, and ice cream flavor are the easiest. Another way of adding variety to a meal is to play a game at the table: Twenty Questions, Whispered Words, One-third of a Ghost, and so forth. Let a grandchild be in charge of manners (this will bring out the best in kids).

5. Vary the seating arrangement. Put a grandchild at the head of the table. Let him pretend to be Grandpa. Or let everyone change seats just before dessert.

One grandfather insists on always sitting next to the baby and shoveling in the baby foods. It seems he missed out on that with his own family and really enjoys it now.

6. Have grandchildren plan the menu in advance. You'll be surprised what you are asked to prepare! And you'll get some good ideas as to what the grandchildren like.

7. When serving new foods, be gentle in your approach. Make it a house rule that a grandchild can ask for a "Royalty Serving" (one tablespoon). But this amount *is* to be eaten. You may find that the next time, he'll eat a normal serving.

8. Make the meal secondary to another event. Go for a long walk, attend a movie or sporting event, look at old family movies, and then eat. When you have an activity first, it makes for good conversation afterwards.

Overnights

What a treat to stay overnight at the grandparents' house! For many grandparents in my survey, a forty-eight-hour visit was considered the ideal length of time. Most grandparents confessed to being exhausted by longer stays, but a few said a long visit was the highlight of their year.

Since such visits are by your invitation, you can set the length that suits you best. Most grandparents prefer to have only one grandchild visit at a time. When one visits, the grandchild is responsive to the grandparent and they get to know each other better. Sometimes one sibling can stifle the other, or they don't get along well—causing worries about tattling to parents. Also, when two grandkids visit, they usually spend more time with each other and less with the grandparents.

Having two grandchildren from different families works well, especially when their interests and ages are similar. Friendships between cousins are one of the blessings of growing up. When cousins don't live near one another, the grandparents may be the catalyst for bringing them together.

Provide a shelf or drawer where a grandchild is allowed to keep a few possessions between visits: pajamas, toothbrush, a toy, books, and other items. This makes going on the overnight less of a hassle. It also makes possible a spur-of-the-moment overnight.

What goes on during these overnights will vary greatly, but don't try to do too much. One major event is sufficient. Don't spend the time racing around town from park to movie to game. Staying up a little later, sleeping late, doing little things together, going on one memorable excursion—that's plenty.

How nice it is when a grandchild returns home from time spent with a grandparent, full of excitement and eager to tell of his adventures.

The Importance of Private Time Together

When a grandparent can have time alone with just one child, the bond becomes closer. They often share secrets. Some grandparents help grandchildren plan a parent's gift for a birthday, anniversary, or holiday. Grandparents can also provide good hiding places for gifts until the occasion for giving comes around.

One grandmother reported that she was the childhood confidante of her grandson and she never betrayed his trust. Early in his life, she let him know that unless he was doing something illegal, she would always try to understand his actions without being judgmental. Through the years he has told her things that worried him, things that weren't going well, even things that he knew to be wrong. She has listened, and sometimes counseled, but mostly listened. He has appreciated this special relationship.

Grandparents, having the perspective of time, often are better counselors than parents, who are sometimes too close to the scene to recognize all the ramifications. There is seldom one right answer to a problem or one right direction to go, and often a grandparent can stand back and suggest many options.

When grandparents were asked their greatest contributions to their grandchildren, more than 82 percent said that love was number one. Many said "unconditional love." Other frequent answers were providing security, being a listening ear, contributing to a sense of family, and encouraging individuality. These contributions aren't made in just one quick visit, but by steady loving interest through the years.

Other Activities at Your House

Try some of these grandchild/grandparent activities:

* One grandfather made a fabulous breakfast when the chaperoned all-night prom party ended. At about six in the morning, parents delivered to his condo twelve graduates, including his granddaughter. He provided fresh-squeezed orange juice, made-to-order omelets, hashed brown potatoes, and sausages.
* Because her grandchildren lived in a townhouse and had no room for a garden, one grandmother provided all the space they

needed in her back yard. She gave them a key to the garage storage so they could come and go as they pleased. Her only request was that the garden be watered as necessary, weeded monthly, and the produce picked before it spoiled.

* Living near the high school was an advantage for one grandmother. Her grandchildren knew that they were welcome to drop in unexpectedly (she'd tell them if she was busy) and that hot chocolate and cookies (kept in the freezer for such occasions) would be served along with a little chat. She was known as "Grandma" by half the sophomore class.

* When the Camp Fire group needed a meeting place, the porch at one grandparents' home was a natural. With the adult leader, certain simple rules were set down for the weekly get-togethers so that it was no work for the hosts. All they ever heard were the sounds of laughter and an occasional flushing toilet. The leader took full charge. When the group went home, the porch was left in perfect order.

* Because grandpa had an empty stall in his garage, two grandsons were given permission to use it for the transformation of a heap of non-functioning metal into a vintage car. The project took over a year, and grandpa kept a big tarp to throw over the project so he didn't have to look at it all the time. The grandfather was occasionally a kibitzer, and he learned a few things himself. He was the first to ride in the vehicle when it was finally roadworthy.

When Grandkids Work for You

Work of the paid and unpaid varieties is sometimes a good link between the generations. If details of the work assignment, including completion time, are clearly understood in advance, the job offer can bless both sides.

Occasionally there are home maintenance tasks that a grandparent doesn't have the skills or strength to do. Recently widowed grandmothers have learned how to change faucet washers via lessons from their grandchildren. Grandfathers have learned how to shop and cook for themselves, thanks to the help of their grandchildren. Others have used grandkids to change storm windows and screens, paint fences, serve at parties, act as chauffeur, help cook meals, and even aid in income tax preparation.

One busy grandmother kept a little list of non-urgent tasks that needed doing. Grandchildren who stopped in would see the list, and the tasks were accomplished along with a friendly chat or an occasional snack.

For most grandchildren, paid work is important. Grandparents should consider their own and the child's financial circumstances before making an offer. It's a good idea to check with parents to be sure that the job won't take time from important school work or home activities. Tell the price you are willing to pay, or the hourly work rate, before starting the project.

One granddaughter spends a late afternoon every other week driving her grandmother to appointments, on errands, and shopping. They have a wonderful time together. Since the granddaughter doesn't have her own car, her "pay" for this service is the use of grandma's car one day a week.

It's up to you just how much your home will become a second home for your grandchildren, a place for camaraderie and for comfort. But don't put off the fun of making your home a place the grandkids love. Remember, what you found with your own children: the growing up years go fast. Enjoy them while you can.

GRANDPARENTS' WORKSHOP

Easy Recipes for Three Generations

How true the commercial that says, "Nothing says lovin' like something from the oven." Here are foods you can make with the help of your grandchildren, or make and take to their home. Don't serve them all at one meal. Use just one at a time to provide new tantalizing taste treats.

These recipes are quick and easy to do. Your grandchildren can learn to make them for you, and thus save you time. The ingredients are moderate in cost, but the taste experience is top rank.

Each recipe was submitted by a grandparent, aunt, or uncle, and was tested in my own kitchen.

*   *   *

The Appetizer: **Grandma Betty's Chutney Cheese Mold**
—it sounds unusual; it tastes wonderful!

1 8 oz. package of cream cheese, softened
1 cup (4 oz.) cheddar cheese, grated
1 hard boiled egg, chopped fine
1/2 small onion, chopped fine
1 teaspoon curry powder
3 tablespoons mayonnaise
1 small jar of mango chutney (or other variety if mango is
  not available)

Mix all ingredients together except chutney. Press into oiled mold. Refrigerate at least one hour, or up to two days. Unmold to serve. Spread chutney over the top. Serve with crackers.

*   *   *

The Main Dish: **Grandma Joyce's Baked Chicken**
—it bakes all afternoon, giving you free time.
(Serves 8)

4 chicken breasts, halved, boned, and skinned (8 pieces)
1/2 pound bacon, uncooked, at room temperature
1 5 oz. jar of dried beef
1 cup sour cream
1 can cream of mushroom soup

Line bottom of 9″ by 13″ pan with chipped beef, slightly overlapping the pieces. Wrap chicken into bundles with bacon and arrange on top of beef. Blend sour cream and soup and pour over the top. Bake at 275 degrees for four to five hours.

* * *

The Vegetable: **Auntie Jessie's Mediterranean Mix**
—a colorful vegetable everyone will love!

1 cup of yellow pepper strips (red or green can be substituted, but yellow looks best)
1 cup zucchini slices
1/2 cup red onion rings
1/2 teaspoon dried oregano, crushed
1 tablespoon margarine, melted
1/2 cup cherry tomatoes cut in halves
3/4 cup (about 6 oz.) crumbled feta cheese

Combine first five ingredients in a casserole or microwave dish. Microwave on high for 4 minutes, stirring after 2 minutes. (Or saute on cooktop until crisp/tender.) Add tomatoes. Microwave (or saute) for one additional minute. Top with cheese.

* * *

The Potato Dish: **Grandpa Cliff's Make-ahead Mashed Potatoes**
—At last, mashed potatoes that aren't a last minute hassle!
(Serves 8 to 12)

5 pounds baking potatoes
1 8 oz. package of cream cheese
1 cup sour cream
1 tablespoon garlic salt
Butter or margarine

Peel and boil potatoes until soft. In a large mixing bowl, use the electric mixer to cream the cream cheese. Add the sour cream. In a separate bowl, mash the potatoes until there are no lumps. Add the sour cream mixture and the garlic salt and mix well. Spread in a large flat casserole and dot with butter or margarine. At this point, the potatoes can be covered and refrigerated for up to 48 hours. Or they may be frozen and thawed before use. Bake at 400 degrees for about 50 minutes until hot and slightly brown on top.

*   *   *

The Dessert: **Grandma Sally's Chocolate Sundae Pie**
—you can vary this with lemon pudding (instead of chocolate pudding).
(Serves 10-12)

Crust:
1 cup all-purpose flour
1 stick (1/4 pound) butter or margarine
2 cups chopped pecans or walnuts

Mix together and press into a greased 9" by 13" pan. Bake at 350 degrees for 20 minutes. Cool.

Filling:
1 cup powdered sugar
1 8 oz. package of cream cheese
1 12 oz. container of prepared whipped cream, divided in half
1 package of chocolate instant pudding
1 package of vanilla instant pudding
2 2/3 cups milk
Grated chocolate (Use baking chocolate or a chocolate candy bar.)

Mix powdered sugar and cream cheese together. Add only 6 oz. of the whipped cream. Spread in pie shell. Then mix together the two pudding powders. Mix in the milk. Spread on top of the first mixture. Top with the remaining 6 oz. of whipped cream. Sprinkle grated chocolate on top. Refrigerate for at least two hours before serving.

*   *   *

The Salad: **Grandma Marj's Napa Cabbage Salad**
—an all time favorite, but no one believes it's cabbage!
(Serves 8 to 12)

Salad:
1 large Napa or similar-style Chinese cabbage
5 green onions

Chop cabbage and onions fine (a food processor shredding disk works well). Cover tightly and chill overnight.

Crunchies:
(Can be made ahead and kept in the freezer.)
2 packages "Top Ramen" soup noodles
2 tablespoons sesame seeds
1 stick (1/4 pound) margarine
1/2 cup slivered almonds

Pre-heat oven to 350 degrees. Melt margarine in a rectangular baking pan. Break the noodles into very small pieces. Add the noodles, seeds and nuts to margarine and toss slightly. Bake until slightly brown, stirring once or twice. (About 10 minutes, but watch carefully.)

Dressing:
1/2 cup salad oil
1/2 cup cider vinegar
2 teaspoons soy sauce
1/2 cup sugar

Mix all together in a jar. Can be made ahead and refrigerated.
Just before serving, add crunchies to greens and toss with dressing. Cooked chicken chunks can be added to make a main dish salad.

*   *   *

The Rolls: **Grandma Nancy's Quick Sticky Biscuits**
—wonderful for breakfast, lunch, or dinner!
(Makes 16 rolls)

Rolls and Filling:
2 cans refrigerated crescent rolls
1/2 cup (firmly packed) brown sugar
1/2 cup chopped nuts
1/4 cup (half a stick) margarine, melted
1 teaspoon vanilla flavoring

Topping:
1/2 cup (firmly packed) brown sugar
2 teaspoons flour
1 tablespoon milk
1/2 teaspoon vanilla flavoring
1/4 cup (half a stick) margarine

Prepare topping: place ingredients in a small sauce pan and heat until mixture comes to a boil. Spoon into sixteen ungreased muffin cups. Next, combine ingredients for the roll filling: brown sugar, nuts, vanilla and margarine. Unroll the triangles of dough and spread mixture on each. Roll up. Cut rolls in half crosswise and place cut side down in the muffin cups on top of the topping. Bake at 375 degrees for 15 to 20 minutes. When rolls are golden brown, take from oven and immediately invert pans onto a cookie sheet. Remove muffin pans after about one minute. Serve rolls warm or cool.

*　　*　　*

The Punch: **Uncle Cameron's Elegant Holiday Punch**
—a real three-generation favorite.
(Serves 8-10)

3 cups apple juice
1 cup milk
1/3 cup sugar
1 teaspoon vanilla
A dash of salt and of nutmeg
2 cups heavy cream, whipped

In advance, combine all ingredients except whipping cream. Before serving, fold in whipping cream.

*　　*　　*

The Supper Dish: **Grandma Caryl's Swiss Family Fondue**
—wonderful for a casual conversational evening.
(Serves 6)

1/4 cup chopped onion
2 teaspoons all-purpose flour
6 slices bacon or 2 tablespoons margarine
4 cups (16 oz.) shredded cheese (jack or cheddar—expensive
   fondue cheese isn't needed)
2 cups sour cream
1 teaspoon Worcestershire sauce
French bread, cut into bite-sized chunks

Cook bacon until crisp. Crumble and set aside. Reserve 2 tablespoons of the drippings. If you don't wish to use bacon drippings, melt 2 tablespoons of margarine in a large saucepan. Cook onion until tender, but not brown. Blend in flour, then Worcestershire. Before serving, blend in cheese and cook over low heat, stirring continuously, until cheese melts. Slowly add sour cream. Do not boil. Place mixture in fondue pot and top with bacon crumbles. Using forks, spear bread, dip in cheese. Serve with a crisp salad for a filling meal.

*   *   *

The Fastest Cake in the West: **Aunt Berit's Wondercake**
This one is quick to make—and it disappears quickly because it's so good.

2 eggs
1 can of cherry pie filling
1 box of chocolate cake mix
1 container of prepared chocolate frosting

Preheat oven to 350 degrees. Grease a rectangular (9″ by 12″) baking dish. In a large bowl beat two eggs. Stir in (by hand) the pie filling and the cake mix. (Do not add any of the ingredients on the cake mix package.)

When mixture is well blended, pour into baking dish and bake for about 25 minutes. Test center for doneness. Frost with the prepared frosting when still warm.

*   *   *

Next time you're feeding the family, surprise them with one of these ten easy recipes. Let your grandchildren help you cook, clean up, and enjoy your culinary creation.

Five

THE FIFTH COMMANDMENT:

You shall add joy and good memories to the lives of your grandchildren

Dear Grandma,

Our four grandchildren—ages five to fifteen—seem so serious about everything. While I think it is wonderful they're concerned with the environment and world hunger, shouldn't there still be time for innocence, laughter, and nonsense in their lives? Our daughter works and so I'm going to give the birthday party for our ten-year-old grandson. Isn't it still acceptable for families to have some silly fun?

PUZZLED PARTY-GIVING GRANDMOTHER

A resounding yes! I'm a party-lover, too. Some of the best and happiest memories of growing up come from happy get-togethers and excursions.

Certainly we should take the world's problems seriously. We teach our children and grandchildren how to defend themselves from the devastations of substance abuse and AIDS, and the heartbreaks of premature sex and pregnancy. We show them how to be safe wherever they are. We educate them about littering and polluting the environment. We encourage awareness of the world's challenge to overcome illiteracy, poverty, hunger and political oppression.

But at the same time we want to encourage joy. Sometimes parents are so busy feeding and directing their kids that they forget the importance of making the home a happy place. As wise King Solomon said: "A merry heart maketh a cheerful countenance: but by sorrow of the heart the spirit is broken. . . . He that is of a merry heart hath a continual feast" (Prov. 15: 13, 15 KJV).

It can be one of the many jobs of a grandparent to encourage this joyful unbroken spirit and merry heart in children. Our very attitude toward certain subjects affecting grandchildren can foster this. Let's remember that grandparents have finished all the hard work of raising, educating, correcting, and financing their own children. Now grandparents can concentrate on building happy memories with their grandchildren.

This "commandment" will consider small and large joyful events, parties, trips, and traditions. These are not selfish activities—treats just for ourselves—but rather events that help a youngster grow into a mentally whole and happy person who can then help others along the way.

One question in my survey was concerning what grandchildren liked most about the time spent with grandparents. At the top of their lists was having fun together. Just being together is important—the when and where are secondary.

Yet many families get into arguments over which holiday is spent with which relatives. Grown daughters are pitted against fathers-in-law and sons are lobbying against sweet grandmas. Fairness is the simple answer because there are plenty of holidays to go around. If the family gathers at one location for Christmas, the other side of the family gets Thanksgiving. The next year they switch. Or maybe they can all get together under one roof. Sometimes there can be a succession of family parties over the holidays. The important thing is to share the holidays as equally as possible, to plan in advance, to not get offended, and never to allow this issue to develop into a family argument. The actual date isn't as important as the getting together. So, in keeping with King Solomon's advice, let's investigate merriment.

The Merry Person

Just what makes a person fun to be with? While there are many answers, certain qualities are common in happy people. See how many of these qualities are ones you practice—or ones you can add to your list of abilities.

* *Flexibility.* At your home, as opposed to the grandchild's home, things do *not* always have to be done at a specific time or in a certain order or manner. Be prepared for the unusual. Expect change. Welcome variety. Be willing to go along with a child's whims. It's okay to occasionally have the dessert first and the meat and potatoes later. Or perhaps the music at dinner will be Springsteen rather than Sibelius. It's equally okay to bend the strict bedtime routine. At your house, when you're in charge, you certainly wouldn't want to undermine the parent's aims, but you can be less rigid. You won't spoil a child, you'll just illustrate that there is more than one good way to accomplish something.

* *Creativity.* At a grandchild's home, the "have-to" list takes precedence over the "want-to" list. But at your house there can be time for creativity. Creativity often ends up at the bottom of a child's list with homework, chores, after-school lessons and sports, and TV consuming all the time. At your house, the racing car track can go under the sofa and through the kitchen and out the back door. . . . The patio can become the artist's studio with lots of room for drippy painting. . . . A hole can be dug in the backyard and a time capsule buried. When a grandchild asks if she can do

something creative, have the "why not?" attitude and try to say yes as often as possible.

* *Conspiracy.* Teach this important word to your grandchildren when they are young. It means a secret plan—and the secrecy does not mean it's unlawful. Conspiracy can be both legal and fun. Maybe you'll conspire with a grandchild to have a surprise party for a classmate, or kidnap a parent and take him to the lake for an hour of relaxing fun, or even clean the parents' garage while they are away. Kids love secrets, so try to have some secret plan in process all the time! It's one more bond between you and your grandchild.

* *Adulation.* Here's a special word to teach your grandchildren. We all flourish with praise and compliments. Grandparents should take pride in their grandchildren's achievements, whether the achievement is large or small. And beyond the pride comes adulation: expressing abundant appreciation. At supper, give toasts: "To Jessica, the best toy picker-upper I know." "To Paul, for raising a C in math to a B-minus." "To Whitney, for making the soccer team." If you're not on hand, write your praise and send it to your grandchild. Kids cherish compliments, and written adulation can be kept and read and reread.

* *Silliness.* While you wouldn't act up at church or at a movie, a little silliness is great in the car (if you aren't the driver), at dinner, while playing a game, or while doing chores. When I was young and helping my grandmother cook, she made it fun in many ways. One way was to ask regularly: "How much pepper should I add?"—even if we were making cherry pie or chocolate pudding. I still smile when I use pepper. Encourage the outlandish side of life with silly sayings, silly stories, even silly clothes. One grandfather has garish red-flowered suspenders that he wears for supper, and the grandkids love to sit in his lap and pull on them.

* *Relaxation.* In these rushed and often tense times, we need to be ardently interested in some things and laid-back about others. Adults often send the message that a good kid is one who knows how to pick-up her room, control the volume of music, or apply the minimum amount of makeup. While those things may have value, they aren't the real essence of youth. Grandparents can teach kids a

71

sense of balance by not overreacting to minor events. And grandparents can show how to make some tasks fun.

One grandmother suggests using relaxed responses. When a grandchild says that something is misplaced, she says: "I don't know where it is, but let's go on safari and find it together." Or when she's asked a homework question and she doesn't know the answer: "I don't know, let's see what Mister Encyclopedia has to say." Or when it's time for bed: "I give you my royal permission to stay up three minutes and thirty seconds longer." Or when a grandchild plays music with particularly obnoxious words: "Those words are about as sensible as songs we sang that said 'Cement Mixer, put-ti put-ti' or 'Mairzy Doats' or 'Hey! Ba-ba-re-bop.' " A relaxed and non-judgmental attitude makes simple everyday events fun both for herself and for her grandchildren.

Merry Moments

Happiness starts by enjoying small moments together. Happiness grows by singing to a baby and making him smile, gasping over a toddler's tall tower of building blocks, applauding the ballerina's first recital, admiring a granddaughter's first earrings or a grandson's first motorcycle—these moments linger happily in memory.

Don't forget to use "Remember when . . . " and recall happy times from the child's past. This is especially important when a grandchild is experiencing disappointment or sadness. Bring back a happy memory. "Remember when we floated paper boats in the flood in the basement? That was a bad day, but we made it fun." "Remember when we thought the cat was lost on Christmas Day and how happy we all were to find that someone had just accidentally shut her in a cupboard in the workshop—she just meowed until we found her."

One grandfather calls his teen granddaughter and asks for "a date" for lunch. It's a small expense (and he says he's learning to like pizza), but it's long on good memories shared.

A grandmother takes her young grandchildren on "look and see" walks. They take along two bags. One bag is called the "basura bag." *Basura* is Spanish for rubbish. In it goes the litter they find along the way. They use a sharp stick to pick up the trash so little hands don't have to touch it. The second bag is the "tesora bag." *Tesora* is Spanish for treasure. In this bag they put a pretty fallen leaf, an interesting stone, a dandelion from a vacant lot—whatever the finders deem worthy of treasure status. When they get home, they put the basura bag in the rubbish, but they display on a patio table all the contents of the tesora bag.

Another grandmother celebrates April Fool's Day with harmless pranks at her house. She colors the milk with safe green food dye. A soft drink has a plastic ice cube with a fake bug imbedded in it. On top of a door that's sure to get closed is a paper cup half filled with water. In a drawer she hides an alarm to go off late in the evening. And she has many more tricks up her sleeve that make for fun and surprises on this "day of foolishness."

None of these merry moments is costly. All it takes is the time to think "What would be fun to do?" or "What would my grandchild enjoy?" and then to do it.

Merry Parties

Many parties are keyed to holidays such as Easter or Thanksgiving, but you don't need to have an official holiday to have fun. Make up a holiday when you think one is needed. Celebrate Broccoli Week, Pet's Day, Laziness Day, and so forth.

One family has a three-generation Super Bowl Party. The guests dress as if going to a game. There's lots of good food and at least two television sets going. The avid fans usually stick to one and don't want to be disturbed even during half-time. Like robots they never take their eyes from the screen, they speak only in grunts, and thrive on replays and commentator opinions. But most of the group takes it less seriously and they have the greater amount of fun, with a wide variety of guessing games and prizes that are awarded about every fifteen minutes.

Another family has a party-by-mail. A few weeks before the night of the Motion Picture Academy Award presentations, all family members are sent ballots for voting in the various categories, and are encouraged to see most of the nominated movies. The grandparents are the official scorekeepers for the evening, giving points for each correct guess. In their separate homes, the television program is watched, but they phone one another during the dull moments. At the end of the evening, the grandparents telephone the top three guessers with their congratulations.

For gradeschool kids, one grandmother gives an end-of-the-school-year party for her grandchildren. Each gets to invite one friend. Since school is out at noon, she and one parent pick them all up for the celebration at a popular restaurant. She brings along fortune cookies for each person and says the fortunes are a humorous prediction of what will happen during the coming summer vacation.

Grandparents' Day in the autumn is another occasion for a family get-together. At this party, which honors the senior generation, one grandparent handed out cards that said, "When I'm a grandparent I am going to . . . " for each person to fill in. These unsigned cards were turned in, shuffled, and then read one at a time. The group tried to guess which person had written the card. After the fun, the grandparents kept the cards as suggestions for activities they might try.

Merry Birthdays

With many families of two away-at-work parents, more grandparents are taking on this annual celebration that means so much to a child. If this falls to you, don't be intimidated. The traditional birthday party that you knew so well is coming back into vogue.

Many parents observe that youngsters are becoming bored with having to sit and watch hired clowns or attend parties at kid-oriented restaurants. Birthdays where kids play games and win prizes are regaining popularity. While these active parties are more work for the giver, they can also be more fun. Best of all, they're less costly! My book *1001 Things to Do with Your Kids* (Abingdon Press, 1988) has sections on both party themes and games to play.

When pre-teen youngsters were asked what elements make a birthday party fun, their answers were revealing. In first place was good prizes. Second was good games. And in third was the right people. Note that elaborate party themes and exotic foods weren't even mentioned.

However, the list is different for teens. First was the party food, then the right people, and finally the party theme.

So, depending on the age of your grandchild, the parties you help plan will differ. Certainly consultation with the party honoree is number one on your list. If your grandchild gives input and has, within reason, the final say on decisions and details, the party will probably be a success.

Adults should avoid these party pitfalls:

1. Being too evident at the beginning and end of the party.
2. Running the party in an obvious way.
3. Rushing the party from event to event.
4. Correcting the guests—unless absolutely necessary for safety.
5. Being concerned about neatness or manners.
6. Attempting to be the life of the party.
7. Engineering the games so that certain kids win.
8. Commenting on the gifts given.

If you can't do those things, what *can* you do? First, plan games that are fun, and FUN is the key word. No matter what the age, don't let the games be too intellectual. Follow this easy rule: if a pencil is involved, the game probably isn't fun because it's too much like homework or a test. Good old games such as Sardine, Balloon Volleyball, and relays are still the best. Start with the most active games so that keyed-up kids use up their excess energy. Then play more passive games where kids take turns.

Next, have lots of prizes. Some prizes should be for the winners. Then have a grab-bag of lesser prizes so that everyone wins. For younger kids, quantity rather than quality is important.

If you are involved in preparing the invitation list, be as inclusive as possible. With teens, insist on a guest list and a "no crashing" rule. Be firm about the guests staying at the party, rather than leaving and coming back (often a sign of trouble, such as drinking or drug use).

For all ages, the food should be simple (and recognizable). Portions should be small, with lots of seconds readily available for big appetites. This is no time to insist on clean plates. Just hope for good manners, but please hold your tongue when there are spills. Clean up quietly and quickly. No matter how old the child is, ice cream and cake with candles is still a favorite routine.

If it falls to you to organize some games, be prepared with the necessary props. Make the rules simple. Explain the rules twice (sometimes let younger kids go through it once as an example). See that games are played fairly and give many opportunities to win. Let the birthday child award prizes.

For a large party you will want additional adult help. A second or third adult is a real help, but you can make this person seem less like the police force if he doubles as photographer. Polaroid cameras are great since party participants can take home pictures of themselves in action.

Plan an activity for both the start and end of the party: one that kids can join as they arrive (since they will come at different times) and drop out as they leave. An obstacle course is a good option for all ages, as it can be done outside or inside. Participants run the course and are timed, the fastest being the winner. Depending on the age of the participants, make the course easy or difficult. Have boxes to climb through, a short rope to climb, a collection of blocks or boxes to stack, a big jump suit to put on and take off again, a paper glass of water to drink, and so on. Everyone finishing gets a prize; the fastest gets the grand prize.

Grandparents are great at party-giving because they can reach back into their past and come up with good old games that can be given new names. For example, Pin the Tail on the Donkey becomes Pin the Tail on the Tyrannosaurus. Limbo, the game where participants must go *under* a pole without knocking it off its props, is now called Space Walking. It's a great game for all ages, no matter what it's called.

If you're in charge, remember to be flexible and try a game or two yourself. The kids will probably get a good laugh watching granddad Space Walk!

A Merry Thanksgiving

One of the most enjoyable times in our family is at Thanksgiving, when our three-generation extended family of children, relatives, and proxy relatives gathers for a party that lasts several days.

The highlight is a semi-structured Thanksgiving Day celebration—the other parties and sports events come spontaneously in the days afterwards. Those who find it impossible to attend have told me how sad they were to have missed one of the happiest get-togethers of the year. These parties have been taking place since our children were small, and now the third generation is learning the joys of family togetherness.

I'm going to tell you quite a bit about our own Thanksgiving Day party. But, if another holiday suits your family better, these ideas can all be readily adapted to another date—with or without turkey.

Because everyone shares the cooking responsibilities, the meal clean-up, and the gentle supervision of little ones, the party flows smoothly for the hosts. There can be thirty people in the house and yard, but I never feel burdened. Events on subsequent days of the long weekend are held at various other homes. However, the Saturday turkey-tacos volleyball game is a return visit to our house, since we have a handy volleyball field—and the left-over turkey.

Lots of photos are taken of this event and exchanged in the weeks that follow, stretching out the memories over a longer period of time. Our family scrapbook for the past year is shared, and everyone enjoys seeing how they looked twelve months before. Clothing is very informal. Alternate activities are provided for young children. But the fun of just being together is the focal point.

These are some of the events we include each year:

1. Surfer's Breakfast. It used to be that you had to be a dripping-wet surfer to attend, but now anyone who loves blueberry muffins and cheesed eggs turns up for this very informal 9:00 A.M. gathering in the living room.

2. Thursday Morning Church Service. Here's the only time for less sporty clothing. The highlight of the service is the informal sharing of gratitude for blessings received during the year. Family members of various faiths gather at one church for this service.

3. The Photo. While everyone is "looking good" after church, we take a group photo. Our pets, as well as visiting pets, are included as essential family members. Every fourth year we take the official family photo that shows off the newest spouses and babies. But the yearly photos include all relatives plus the "honorary" aunts, uncles, and cousins who have been invited this particular year.

4. The Volleyball Championship. This is a best-of-three-games competition. The group is divided into two teams, balancing better players with novices. Some prefer to be alternate players, cheerleaders, or ball-fetchers. And some are entertaining little folk or putting the finishing touches on the big meal.

5. The Feast. Here is the traditional meal with autumn table decor, place cards, and grace given by a different person each year. (One year it was given in Swedish, another time in American Sign Language, but it's always heart-warming.) For this buffet I make the turkey and stuffing and others bring the many potato, vegetable, salad, and relish dishes. Some families carry special food contributions across the country, while other out-of-towners make their dishes the night before at the various places they are housed. And a few collegiates (who get easier food assignments) have been known to stop by the supermarket on their way to the feast!

6. Favors. Since we don't exchange birthday or Christmas gifts with many of these people, there is a favor at each place. It's fun to search for this one gift during the year and buy it in quantity. Little porcelain houses, candlesticks, small photo frames, and tiny crystal trees have been some of the favorites. Young children don't get the favor, but instead a hands-on toy for play later in the day.

7. Awards. Between the meal and dessert, we have a breather for awards. Amusing prizes are given for the first to RSVP by phone and the first by mail, youngest and oldest at the table, kids with clean plates, and so forth. Credits—and applause—are also given to the various cooks who prepared the feast.

8. Gratitude Time. Everyone has an opportunity to share something special from the past year: a new job, a problem solved, a graduation, a wedding, a special trip, or some noteworthy progress in the world. And we discuss the historic significance of this holiday. One year the grade-school kids put on a skit of the first Thanksgiving, which was more hysterical than historical. The most memorable moment came when someone stepped on the turkey's crepe paper tail and the entire costume fell off!

9. Annual Funny Story Contest. Along with the invitation to the yearly event comes the yearly reminder to bring a joke or story. Two attendees (usually two who forgot to bring a story) act as judges. We go around the table and tell our stories and hope for big laughs and applause. Sometimes there has to be a "joke-off" to settle the winner. Joke calendars for the new year—the kind that feature popular cartoonists and are available at bookstores—are the traditional prizes. Then dessert is served.

10. Resting Time. After the pie and the customary "I ate too much" comments, everyone engages in different activities. Of course, there has to be kitchen clean up and dishes readied for the evening meal. Some return for a grudge game on the volleyball court. Others want a nap. But the most popular is the Thanksgiving walk that makes everyone feel less guilty about all the food eaten. Babies in strollers, oldsters with canes, and dogs on leashes make a steady stream through the neighborhood.

11. Photo Contest. Each person has been reminded in the invitation to bring the "best photo" of the year. These are tacked up on a big board for all to admire. Everyone, including babies, gets two votes each (so you can vote for your own and one other). Yes, all the kids vote. In the case of a baby, the parents hold the baby up to the photo board and through various methods determine the baby's choice. Photos that have won include wedding pictures, baby photos (naturally), a landscape from an Alaska canoe trip, and even a sonogram of an unborn baby! A photo frame or album is the usual prize.

12. The New Game. Each year, someone comes up with a new game to try. Sometimes the game is a winner, sometimes a loser. But everyone gives the new game a fair chance. It's a good way for the grandparent generation to broaden their game education. In many trivia games, age is a benefit and teams fight to get the older relatives on their teams.

13. Piñata Bashing. This is often thought of as a kids-only game, but everyone in our family loves it. (A piñata is a large decorated container for candy. If you can't buy one where you live, you can make one out of cardboard and crepe paper.) Usually piñatas are available in animal shapes such as peacocks, dogs, or elephants, but no matter what ours is, it is always called a turkey (much to the confusion of the little folks who know their animals). Wrapped candy is placed inside. It is hung outside at the garage door on a rope attached to a pulley. We draw numbers to determine who goes first. The person who is to "bash the turkey" is blindfolded, turned around three times, handed a bat and told to swing. Of course, those operating the pulley are making the target turkey go up and down so that most swings just hit empty space. The pulley operators are more kind to the little kids, as the piñata can usually sustain some hits and still remain useable. Eventually the candy begins to spill out, but usually not before everyone has had a turn, and then there is a free-for-all.

14. The Snapping Game. This has been our traditional before-supper game for over two decades. In fact, there is a rotating trophy for the winner. The group sits in a circle and numbers off from one to as many as are seated in the circle. Number one is the leader, and the object is to get to be number one. The leader starts and others join with this rhythmic routine: two slaps on the thighs, two hand claps, a snap with the right-hand fingers and then a snap with the left. On the right-hand snap, the leader calls his own number (one) and on the left-hand snap, he calls any other number (for example, eight). The rhythmic slap/slap, clap/clap, snap/snap continues but this time number eight must call (without hesitation) his own number on the right snap and another number on the left snap. The pace starts slowly, but increases as the game goes on. There may be many calls and answers before someone makes a mistake. If a player fails to respond on time to the call or forgets his number, the game stops, he goes to the highest numbered place in the circle, and others move up one chair. Thus, depending where in the line-up the mistake was made, many get a new lower number to remember. Since everyone makes mistakes in this fast-paced game, there is plenty of opportunity to move into the number one seat—and be deposed shortly thereafter. As the preparations for the evening meal conclude, the players are given a three-minute warning and the person who is number one at the end of that time is declared the winner.

15. The Evening Meal. This very informal meal is made more glamorous by candlelight. Again, the food duties are shared. Everyone sits in a different place than at the midday feast. One nephew always makes several loaves of homemade bread in the afternoon to go with the turkey for sandwiches. New salads join leftovers. Two attendees bring plates of cookies for dessert.

16. More Prizes. At this meal, the winners of the yearly best photo contest are announced, and the snapping game winner is honored. Again there is applause for the evening cooks. Once more everyone pitches in for the clean-up.

17. Best Home Video. The traditional closing event is a video presentation compiled by my husband. All during the year he searches the channels for unique stand-up comics, memorable historic footage, and other items of general interest. This is compiled into a 20-30 minute presentation. Everyone stretches out on the floor in front of the TV to see it.

Singing around the piano, meaningful and not-so-meaningful

conversation, baby holding, and all the previously described events have now filled an entire day. Plans begin to be made for other long-weekend get-togethers and the Saturday volleyball game. But some families will be leaving sooner.

So the farewells begin. But the memories of a really joyful celebration linger in thought and tide us over until we all meet again.

Merry Traditions

Every family has traditions like our Thanksgiving ones. It is often the grandparents who keep these traditions alive and well, providing happy memories. Here are some other traditions shared by grandparents who took part in my survey:

* *First long dress.* One grandmother makes it known well in advance that she wants to buy the first long dress for each of her granddaughters. She's invited on the shopping expedition, of course. If you do this, you may want to give the recipient an advance idea of how much you're willing to spend.

* *Four-year-old toolbox.* One grandfather gives a special gift when a grandchild is four-years-old. It is a real (not a toy) toolbox—given to both girls and boys. In the box are two or three simple tools. New tools are given as gifts on other occasions. He also provides the how-to lessons so that these young people can safely use the tools. This grandad says his thirty-year-old grandson still has the box and tools in the garage of his own home.

* *Popcorn and apples.* Grandparents don't always have to serve a big meal when the kids visit. One pair has a traditional Sunday night supper of popcorn and apples with mugs of soup served in front of the fireplace.

* *High Fives.* A fun-loving grandad has taught all his wee grandtots how to give "high fives" when meeting and parting.

* *First car.* Two grandparents, who are a bit more affluent than most, have made an offer their grandkids find irresistible. They offer to match (up to a set limit) the child's earnings for the purchase of the first car. It's a good incentive to get those wheels!

* *Country and Western.* A grand-couple who enjoy dancing have

started the tradition of teaching their grandchildren the fun of square, round, and other folk dances. With a record player and a clean garage floor, they get all the young people involved. (They say even the toddlers like to try it.) This has proven so popular that one teen has invited his friends to join in.

* *The gingerbread house.* Each year, a grandmother and grandson construct a cookie and candy house—complete with garden, people, and pets. The first year they used a kit, but now that they're "pros," they make their own cardboard base. They bake gingerbread cookies for the walls and people and use purchased candy and other cookies for decorating the roof and making the fence and flowers. They have a lot of fun and have become very inventive, but they always take a photo of it before encouraging the family to eat the finished product.

* *First earrings.* A grandmother who understands some of the symbols of growing up, has made a deal with her granddaughters, with the parents' permission. When they are age twelve or older, she takes each granddaughter to a reputable place for ear piercing and the purchase of the first two pairs of earrings.

Such traditions are fun to both contemplate and reminisce about.

Merry Travels

Short excursions and longer trips with grandchildren can be wonderful occasions for three-generation togetherness, but grandparents insist that the best and happiest travels take place when they are alone with their grandchildren.

Before embarking on a trip, grandparents should have an in-depth discussion with grandchildren and their parents. Things that need to be settled are transportation costs, expense money, sleeping arrangements, chaperoned or solo dating while on a trip, and other behavior rules.

Weekend trips are most popular, with one- and two-week trips being next. Longer trips seem tiring and difficult for both grandparents and grandchildren. The benefits of joint travel aren't usually extended by a longer trip.

One set of grandparents has a very marvelous plan for all their grandchildren. Starting when the first grandchild was born, they set aside funds for travel. When a child is old enough to understand, (about age five, they say), they explain that they want to take the child on a trip to honor birthday number twelve.

Twelve is selected as the ideal age for several reasons. There are still some travel cost bargains for this age. A twelve-year-old is old enough to be self-sufficient and safe. Also, this age is not yet into dating, so the grandparents don't have to worry about a teen who moans and mopes and complains she's missing her boyfriend. Also, when the grandchildren are this age, the grandparents usually still feel quite active and able to keep up with a youngster.

The preceding year, the grandparents decide on two or three one- to two-week trips that they themselves would feel happy about making with the child. The grandchild is then given details of each trip so he knows exactly what things he would be seeing and doing. The grandparents don't want any surprises here! After being given several weeks to contemplate the choices, the grandchild makes the selection and the exciting planning begins.

These grandparents include the child in almost all of the planning: visiting the travel agent, seeing a video on sights to be seen, and even reading an interesting novel about the area. They work together to make a list of take-alongs. As the time gets closer, they talk almost daily. When they return, they have a party where they share experiences and show pictures and souvenirs.

Younger siblings look forward to their turn. Older ones speak of what a great treat this was. The grandparents have already done this for five of their seven grandchildren. What a gift!

While the finances of many grandparents wouldn't permit a gift of this magnitude, the idea can be scaled down to meet individual circumstances. A membership in the zoological society and monthly visits together or a week-long fishing and camping trip are other possibilities. But if you are like the famous Auntie Mame, you can just gather up your grandchild and go around the world. Either way, you'll be building happy memories.

GRANDPARENTS' WORKSHOP

Hundreds of grandparents in my survey listed what were the best and happiest times with their grandchildren. Here's a compilation of their top-rated activities. You may want to check off the ones you'd like to try.

- [ ] Card games
- [ ] Camping out in a backyard tent
- [ ] Taking a child out for dinner as a surprise
- [ ] Working together on holiday plans
- [ ] Going to a book sale and buying bargains
- [ ] Doing puzzles
- [ ] Building a tree house
- [ ] Shopping with teens
- [ ] Teaching magic tricks to young children
- [ ] Building and flying kites
- [ ] Surprising grandchildren with an unplanned overnight trip
- [ ] Teaching swimming and diving
- [ ] Visiting a bank, opening a savings account
- [ ] Sharing skills in tennis, golf, horseback riding
- [ ] Baking cookies together and delivering them
- [ ] Surprising a parent with a handmade gift
- [ ] Taking kids to interesting hands-on museums
- [ ] Sitting outside in the dark and talking
- [ ] Taking one grandchild on a vacation
- [ ] Attending a grandchild's performance or sports event
- [ ] Going to a toy store and making a want-list for use later
- [ ] Making a life-size paper cut-out of a young grandchild
- [ ] Teaching a grandchild about computers
- [ ] Reading books together until grandparent and grandchild fall asleep

☐ Teaching a toddler to tie shoes or tell time
☐ Planning a party from start to end
☐ Providing a grandchild with two tickets to an event
☐ Introducing a grandchild to big league baseball
☐ Taking grandkids to see a grandparent's childhood area
☐ Providing pizza and a home video for a grandchild and a few of his friends
☐ Taking a whole day to visit the zoo
☐ Feeding horses and other farm animals
☐ Counting stars
☐ Visiting the Humane Society "just to look"
☐ Playing box games
☐ Repainting the child's room together
☐ Taking a grandchild fishing at dawn
☐ Giving a grandchild one of your own possessions

Six

THE SIXTH COMMANDMENT:

You shall not continually give gifts to your grandchildren

Dear Grandma,

As soon as we see him, our seven-year-old grandson Jacob always says, "What did you bring me, Grandma?" This is probably our own fault since my husband and I usually bring a little gift when we come to visit. We don't give expensive gifts except for birthdays or Christmas, but we try to bring a toy or book when we can. Now we're wondering if we've started something we can't keep up, especially since we have five more grandchildren living in other parts of the country. It's not as easy to be in contact with them and to know what they'd want.

Another problem is that Jacob usually just takes the gift and wanders off, not spending much time with us, except at mealtime. What's going on here?

GIVING GRANNY

What's going on is simply this: you are teaching your grandson that the most important thing about you is a gift. Jacob isn't finding out the more important things about you—your special talents, your good ideas, the exciting history you've lived through, or your interesting present-day activities. Yes, it often seems easier to *buy* something than to *be* something.

Of course, there are occasions for gifts—that's what this chapter is about: when to give, how to give, even what to give. But some grandparents confuse grandparenting with "grandgiving," and that causes problems. Don't try to buy love with gifts. It won't work for very long.

When a child has two sets of grandparents, often one has more money to spend than the other. If you're the ones with more money, you probably also have more free time, so give fewer material things and more of yourself. If you're the ones with less money, don't fret. Wealth isn't a necessity for good grandparenting. Don't try to compete with the other grandparents in this area—or in any area. Be original . . . give the gifts of time and talent first, material gifts second.

Separate but Equal

Most grandchildren firmly believe that the kids who live near their grandparents get lots more gifts. Sometimes that is true. It is so easy to bring a little gift, to give in to a child's requests at the store, to do something extra for that appealing youngster whom you see often.

But remember, kids compare. Certainly it is harder to "gift" far-away grandkids as it means the hassle of packing and the expense of mailing a parcel. But, more difficult, it means trying to know *what* to send. We'll come to that later in this chapter.

Equal treatment doesn't have to be identical treatment. It would be nice to be able to give equal time and equal attention to each grandchild. But that's almost impossible. Be sure that in the magnitude of your gift-giving you don't short-change the out-of-towners. One grandparent didn't believe she was giving more to one grandchild than another until she kept a little list for a year. She wrote down the date, the name of the large or small gift, and the cost. She was amazed that she spent almost twice as much on her in-town granddaughter. "It was just a little here and a little there," she said.

Certainly a grandchild may have a greater need at a certain time in his life. One very generous grandfather makes a small contribution toward house down payments as each grandchild heads for home ownership. He doesn't have to do all this giving in the same year, but it is the same amount each time the need arises. He, too, keeps a ledger of his gifts.

You may be saying, "What difference does it make if we give one grandchild more than another?" It shouldn't make any difference unless the difference is large—and quite evident. But you *do* want to be fair in your giving. Unfortunately, when young people detect a lack of fairness, they often equate it with a lack of love. So you certainly don't want to play favorites.

Devise your own method for fair giving. Not the same toys and gifts, but ones about equal in value and interest to the youngster (some boys don't like clothes gifts, most girls do). And, a vital point: don't make giving such a big deal!

The "What Did You Bring Me?" Syndrome

If you've been the king or queen bearing gifts at each visit, change your method. Certainly bring a gift when you feel like it. "Just because" gifts can be the very best. But don't make it an "every time" event.

Instead of bringing a gift, select something to take along that you can share. Thus prepared, you won't arrive empty-handed. This could be a photo, a book you enjoy with a specially descriptive passage marked, an item you've made, or your favorite recording. Such things can start a dialogue with your grandchild, helping him to appreciate your interests, and helping both of you to become good buddies.

Use part of your money for gifts of a less tangible variety: tickets, excursion admissions, or lessons. These costs mount up, so without being a Scrooge, help your grandchild appreciate the value of the expenditure and the importance of being judicious in spending money.

One grandmother is called "The Book Granny" by her grandsons. She happens to be an avid reader and a library volunteer. Any grandparent could follow her lead. She sees her two grandsons weekly and loves to "gift" them. She has given them one of the greatest gifts: the love of books and reading. At her local library and others nearby, there are yearly book sales where prices are as low as ten cents. So for just a few dollars, she can buy a carton of books that will last for nearly a year. Before each visit, she picks two books that would interest the boys and these books become part of their own personal library. Books that they tire of or grow out of find their way back to the library for someone else to enjoy. At times she gives the kids other gifts, but I think the books are her finest choice.

When the Grandkids Live Far Away

"The Book Granny" inspired me to do something similar. I knew of a military family, with three gradeschoolers, stationed at a remote base in Japan. I went to a library book sale and spent twenty dollars on good-as-new paperback books. I could barely carry the box home! But, thanks to the APO address, the shipping cost was small. I put a note inside the box that these books were well-loved by previous readers, and that they were coming to them for no special occasion, just because I was thinking of them. The prompt and effusive thank-you notes from the kids indicated that this was an idea worth perpetuating.

If you give gifts at unique times, rather than for each and every meeting, they seem more special. We have twenty-four grandnieces and grandnephews. That's a lot of people to buy for! I know they are amply "gifted" for their birthdays and at Christmas time, so we choose to be the Valentine's Day givers. There are many advantages to this. Our gift arrives at a time when it may be the only gift, so it is more appreciated and remembered. The gift wasn't lost in the pile at Christmas. The gift doesn't go on the long list of thank-you notes to write. It's usually the only gift, so the note is more personal. Even months afterward, many of these young people are able to remember the gift and make special mention of it to us.

I can shop for these twenty-four gifts in my leisure after the rush of the holidays. The after-Christmas sales let me give more valuable gifts than I could have afforded to buy earlier. Almost all of these children live far enough away that I must wrap and mail the items so I try to buy lightweight, unbreakable things. One example, colorful nylon duffelbags with their names appliqued, was a great hit with them!

Each year, starting in early February, one astute boy eagerly asks his mother if his Valentine from Aunt Caryl and Uncle Cliff has arrived yet. I like his anticipation of something good coming. I must admit I like the distinction, too!

One grandmother sends a non-chocolate item at Easter. She says that salt-free pretzel sticks are a healthy contrast to all the chocolate bunnies. Another recommends sending a book in time for summer reading. One grandfather makes wooden puzzles and sends them each August when the kids are bored with their vacation leisure. A grandmother provides new pajamas for the grandkids each Christmas Eve. Another doesn't give just one big gift, but rather gives twelve small gifts to open on the twelve days of Christmas.

When you don't live nearby, it's difficult to know what especially interests the grandchildren. But if you've learned the skills of good communication, as described in chapter 1, you will have good ideas on what to send. If you still don't, just ask the parents for suggestions. Or ask your grandchildren to submit a yearly "wish list."

The Wish List

Don't hide behind the "I don't know what they want" excuse. Don't deprive yourself of this wonderful opportunity to connect with your grandchild. Giving should be fun—fun for you to select and buy, fun for you to give, fun for your grandchild to receive.

Some grandparents buy gifts at stores that have easy exchange policies. Others take the grandchildren to the store and let them pick out the gift. I know one grandmother who makes this toy store trip several months before the grandchild's birthday. She takes the gift home, wraps it, and keeps it until the special day. That's real self-control on the part of the grandmother, and the heightened anticipation on the part of the grandchild is good, too. One year the youngster said as he tore open the gift, "Oh, I'm so happy because I've been wanting this *so* long!"

I think the yearly wish list is a good solution. Each year, write your grandchildren a wish list letter. Tell them you would like to provide them with gifts they'd really enjoy. Enclose a stamped postcard with your address on it. Tell the youngsters that they should put on the message side of the card a list of the top items they want. Tell the grandchildren that if the card doesn't come back to you, you assume they want socks (deemed the dullest of gifts by kids). When the cards come back, you then have a handy prepared list to use for those special gift-buying occasions. To avoid duplication, you may want to check with parents before purchasing expensive items.

One family reports that the arrival of grandpa's wish list letter is a highlight since it brings about animated supper table discussion. After the meal there is often very careful printing to be sure that he can read what is wanted.

Don't miss the list of most-wanted gifts at the end of this chapter.

The Family Gift

Many young families nowadays don't have the funds to make certain large purchases. Sometimes, by putting together all the funds you would spend on each member of the family, you're able to buy that one item. I can remember the Christmas that my parents decided to give an outdoor jungle gym set to their grandchildren. They were visiting us from another state, so when they arrived they bought a to-be-assembled set and hid it in the garage.

After the kids had gone to bed Christmas Eve, we four adults gathered in a far corner of the backyard and had the usual frustrating but amusing time getting the thing put together. With two assemblers, one instruction reader, and one refreshments chairman, we finally succeeded. It was worth the pain to see the kids find their gift in the morning. In pajamas and nighties they crawled all over it for hours. It was a very special gift that gave the youngsters pleasure for years. And even today, two decades later, when they see pictures taken that long-ago Christmas morning they comment on this "best-ever gift."

Other big gifts to consider might be a week at camp, computer hardware or software, a good encyclopedia set, volleyball equipment, a Ping Pong table, or a dog with all the necessary fees, equipment, and food. Remember, though, never give a pet without privately checking with the parents in advance.

And Then There Is Money

"I just send checks," said one grandmother. "It takes care of everything easily and quickly. Besides, I don't know what to give." That's an acceptable solution if you are extremely ill, excessively busy, or totally uninterested in your grandchildren.

Most kids like to get *some* cash, but unfortunately a very small percentage of kids make good use of gift money. Often it is merely frittered away. So, as a grandparent, your hard-earned cash gift has had little impact.

A nice compromise is cash *and* gift. Divide your gift budget in half. Use half of the money to buy a gift that you know your grandchild can use. Give the other half in the form of a check. In your card (or in person) say, "I'd like you to let me know what you do with the money." By saying this, you show that you're truly interested in the child's needs.

It goes without saying that when a gift is given, the giver has no more responsibility. If the gift is returned to the store, if it is lost or broken, or if the money is frittered away, it's not up to you to judge or comment. If you find that a youngster isn't appreciating your gift selections, perhaps it's time to find out just what kinds of gifts would please your grandchild.

Some grandparents like to make a gift to a particular fund, such as a grandchild's car fund. When she finally bought her "clunker," one granddaughter told her grandparents: "The back seat is yours; you paid for it!"

Often a grandparent establishes a savings account in a grandchild's name when the child is born. Then, on special occasions, a sum is added to the account. One math-minded grandfather has a deliberately complicated formula for this giving, and he regularly shares it with his grandson to make sure he's keeping up with his arithmetic lessons. The formula is: age divided by two, multiplied by $4.50, plus $1.10 for each grade in school. Thus a ten year old gets $10.00 divided by two ($5.00) times $4.50 ($22.50) plus $5.50 for fifth grade, equalling $28.00. You can be sure the youngster checks the formula carefully each birthday!

Some grandparents also give money for a college fund—and these days that is most welcome. The problem is that a fund for the future sometimes lacks immediate pleasure, especially with a young child. A grandmother remedied this by not only making a contribution to the college savings account, but also giving a book on a particular career. Over the years, her granddaughter was exposed to books on the subjects of jobs in social services, law, medicine, computers, government and foreign services, teaching, marketing, real estate, and fashion design.

One grandparent was giving ten dollars as a gift, but wanted his gift to look festive. He got ten balloons. Before blowing up each of the ten, he inserted a rolled-up dollar bill into the neck of the balloon. Then he blew up the balloons and tied them together with a ribbon. He told his granddaughter she had to sit on each balloon until it broke. When she found the dollar in the first one, she was eager to pop the others.

Do You Get Thanked?

There's the story of the grandchild who was endorsing the gift check and, as his only thank-you note, wrote on the back of the check "Thank you, Grandma." I hope that isn't a true story. Such laziness and lack of appreciation are so sad.

Of course, you don't give a gift in order to be thanked. But it is nice to know that the gift arrived and was appreciated. Teaching kids to write thank-you notes is a parental duty. It's good practice during a child's growing-up years, and this skill will be a great social asset in later years.

Parents who insist on thank-you notes or specific thank-you calls when a child is young are to be commended. This establishes a good habit, and incidentally ensures more gifts through life. There are those grandparents who say they stopped giving because they never were thanked—and who can blame them?

The tradition of saying or writing thanks often comes to a child by inheritance. If the grandparents had insisted on it with their own children, the parents will make their children do it (sometimes just to get even). Youngsters should be taught that writing the thank-you note is part of accepting the gift. If you don't want to write the note, don't accept the gift. In some families it's a tradition to write after-Christmas notes all together. However it comes about, teaching this social grace is important.

A wise grandmother puts a small package of thank-you stationery in her grandson's Christmas stocking each year. Another grandmother had years of trouble getting responses from her granddaughter. She didn't like to call or remind. So, she starting putting a self-addressed return postcard in each gift. Sometimes the message side was blank, sometimes there was a line to be filled in, sometimes a response to be checked off: "The gift arrived: in good condition. in bad condition. I like the gift. I don't like the gift." At least that way she knew it had been received. After a few years of the grandmother's using this not-so-subtle gimmick, her granddaughter said to her, "You don't have to do that anymore, I've grown up now and I know to drop you a note." And she did.

If done with gentle loving kindness and a dose of patience, it's acceptable for grandparents to remind grandchildren that they need to write thank-you notes.

The Gift of Giving

A friend of mine made a very special gift offer to her grandchildren. These three young people were high school and college students at the time, but her offer would work equally well with older or even somewhat younger kids. She wrote them identical letters about a month before Christmas. In the letters, she reminded them of what their parents had done for them, the sacrifices they had made, and the many gifts they had given the kids.

Now, she said, she was going to give these youngsters "The Gift of Giving." She said that for almost two decades she had spent a certain amount of money yearly to buy Christmas gifts for each of them. A check for that amount was enclosed. They were to keep the project secret from their parents, but they were to use the money to buy their parents some very special Christmas presents that year. She suggested that they really give the project some thought and come up with memorable selections. And she said she would like them to write her about the results of "The Gift of Giving."

Since these young people live across the country from the grandparents, she didn't hear about the completion of the project until after Christmas when each of them did write. One who lived at home had been careful to observe his parents' personal needs, and had his packages ready for Christmas morning. One of the collegiates arrived home just in time to take part in the Christmas Eve shopping rush, but enjoyed sharing in the spirit of the season as she spent her sum in the crowded festive stores. The third youngster didn't arrive home until Christmas Day, having been occupied with exams and a short trip, but this was no deterrent. He went to the after-Christmas sales and was able to buy twice as much for each parent *and* treat them to lunch!

My friend says that this shouldn't be an every-year tradition, especially as young people reach the time when they are earning money and want to buy nice gifts for their parents. But the project went so well and the grandchildren were so enthusiastic about it, that she has decided to repeat the idea with some of the younger grandkids.

Don't Just Give the Gift

Package opening is part of the fun. Unfortunately, sometimes the "gifting" seems to be over even before it begins. For most people past the toddler years, part of the fun is savoring each gift. Try these ideas to make giving—and receiving—more memorable:

* *Hot and cold.* This is good for any gift, but especially those hard-to-wrap or hard-to-disguise items. Hide the gift in an out-of-the-way place (garage, closet, attic). Tell the recipient that she's to find the gift with your help, but that the only words you will say are warm/hot/hotter or cool/cold/colder, to indicate going in the right direction, being in the right room, or getting near to the gift. Give hints often for young children, but less often for older ones.
* *Giving is best.* At Christmas, when there are many gifts and givers, emphasize giving rather than receiving. Slow the pace; don't let the wrappings be ripped rapidly, ending the fun of anticipation and leaving kids with no knowledge of who gave what. Emphasize the giving by taking turns being the Santa. This means one person will hand out the gifts at one time to everyone present. Read the gift tag aloud. Open only one gift at a time. Let everyone have a chance to look at it. This helps the receivers to appreciate the giver's selections.
* *Little hints.* Keep the gift hidden. Give the recipient three hints, such as "It's bigger than a breadbox," "It's hidden at knee height," or "It will make you laugh." Then follow the recipient around as she tries to find it.
* *Double gifts.* Put a more interesting gift inside a less interesting one. For example, one grandparent put a much-wanted ring inside

a box of letter paper. A pair of overalls had little toys in every pocket. A book contained an envelope with two tickets to the circus.

* *Delayed gift.* On a child's birthday, there is always great excitement when the gifts are opened. And sometimes there is a let-down later in the day when the party is over. Have one small gift as the last gift of the day. Tuck it under the child's pillow or in with pajamas.

Gifts to Avoid

Your knowledge of your grandchild, her wish list, or information from a parent will give you ideas on good gifts. But sometimes you have to go it on your own instincts. There are traps out there! Some gifts are mostly packaging and advertising hype. Don't waste your money.

Here are some gifts to avoid:

* Toys that simulate violence or encourage violent play (guns, war games, video games that are based on the "success" of blowing away the opposition). Why encourage brutality when there is already so much of it in the world?

* Trendy expensive toys (specific dolls, modern toy guns, name-brand clothes)—you're not getting good value for your money because of heavy advertising and marketing costs. Retain your native skepticism. This year's hyped toy is next year's junk.

* Video games. While these have some value, many are violence-based. They teach aggression and increase tension as the player tries for successive high scores. They take time from active play, making a child an observer, rather than a doer.

* Always dolls for girls, trucks for boys. Boys and girls need both creative and active toys, so don't be sexist.

* A gift that can't be played with or used. Toys that are so precious they must be kept on a shelf aren't advantageous to a young child. Certainly when a youngster reaches the age for collectibles this will change, but in the meantime give gifts that can be enjoyed hands-on.

* Cheap toys with shoddy workmanship and sharp corners. "Play with" (test) the toy yourself before buying.

Each time you're at your grandchild's home, spend a little time in her room or in the family room where she plays. You'll get good ideas for giving when you see the toys and books she enjoys most. Crafts, tools, and truly useful gadgets such as radios are other good gifts. Don't forget that as kids get older, clothes become wanted gifts.

Check your yellow pages directory for school supply stores. They have sturdy toys, intriguing educational games, and fine selections of books. Certain mail-order catalogs also feature quality gifts.

Through the years you'll give many gifts to your grandchildren. Make the selecting fun for yourself and the receiving fun for them.

GRANDPARENTS' WORKSHOP

If you go to the toy store and ask for suggestions, you'll probably be directed to the most popular sellers—the ones being advertised the most. These aren't always the best toys for you to buy. You want something that is fun to use and that will last. A toy that teaches imagination, ingenuity, intelligence, and dexterity is an added plus.

Building blocks, dolls, trucks, box games, records, books—these are stand-bys that come immediately to mind. These can be fine gifts. But here are some other ideas for each age group:

Pre-school children:

1. Magnetic design board (such as Etch-A-Sketch)
2. Sets of plastic animals (farm, ark, stable, zoo)
3. Easel, artist's apron, and art supplies
4. Youth roller skates
5. Small rocking chair
6. Sandbox with cover
7. Simple music box
8. Fabric playhouse to fit over cardtable
9. Masks, hats, simple costumes
10. Molded plastic slide or tunnel
11. Activity balls (non-slip, to sit and even stand on)
12. Safe outdoor swing
13. Carry-case for going visiting
14. Bookshelf
15. Sheets, blanket, or spread with scenic designs
16. Rhythm instruments

Grade-school youngsters:

1. Terrarium
2. A complete costume
3. Bubble wand kit for making huge bubbles in varied shapes
3. A mobile of the planets for hanging in bedroom
4. Magnets of all sizes (or other kits for scientific play)
5. Stamps and inkpad sets

6. Leather or jewelry craft kits
7. Magic tricks
8. Hand-held calculator
9. Puppets and theater
10. Dollhouse with furniture and people
11. Pogo stick
12. Trampoline
13. Sleeping bag
14. Simple camera and film
15. Basketball, basket
16. Equipment for Scouting or other groups

Teens:

1. Luggage, dufflebag
2. Camping or hiking gear, pedometer, compass, cooking kit
3. Guitar or other instrument
4. Address stickers, printed stationery
5. Volleyball and net
6. Waterproof watch
7. Telescope
8. Short-wave radio
9. Kiln and pottery-making supplies
10. Bird, cage, supplies
11. Punching bag
12. Desk lamp
13. Jewelry, jewelry box
14. Photo album
15. Microscope
16. Good pocket knife

Young adults living alone or married:

1. Decorative indoor plant
2. Outdoor barbecue
3. Croquet set
4. Sun lounger
5. Wall hanging, picture
6. Good tools
7. Magazine subscription
8. Gourmet cooking lessons
9. Popcorn maker

10. Desk set
11. Mystery party game kits
12. Clock
13. Stamp dispenser machine
14. Jewelry
15. Picnic basket
16. Binoculars

Seven

THE SEVENTH COMMANDMENT:

You shall use discipline and babysitting authority with great care

Dear Grandma,

I think our grandchildren just wait for us to come over to look after them, and then they do every kind of wild and weird thing they can think of. The parents (our son and his wife) say they don't act up for them, just when we babysit. The kids are ages four through fourteen, and we don't know what to do to keep them in line. Sometimes I feel like just spanking them, but my wife says that's not a modern means of discipline. Well, what's modern that works?

GRANDFATHER-IN-CHARGE

When we are put in charge, we like to *be* in charge! It's frustrating to feel that we're being taken advantage of by anyone, especially our precious grandchildren. Of course, when the parents are on hand, the grandparents don't have to get into the discipline question. But when grandparents babysit, disciplinary matters come up. This is the touchiest area for the three generations. This chapter will consider two topics that are often tied together: babysitting and discipline.

Unless it is a matter of child abuse or illegal behavior, it's wise to keep out of the discipline between parent and child. Perhaps you have some suggestions or some good disciplinary methods you have gleaned through experience or reading. During a private moment with the parents, ask if they'd like to hear your ideas. But don't be surprised if they aren't interested or just listen politely or don't put the ideas into use.

Remember that you had your chance at establishing good habits when you were the disciplinarians for your own child, who is now the parent. No doubt your child vividly remembers some of your methods! Possibly he uses some of them—or perhaps he has purposely decided to do something quite different.

Take into consideration your own successes and failures with your child. Remember that now your child's spouse is also contributing ideas from childhood experiences. When it comes to discipline, each family has to find its own style. Try to be supportive, rather than critical. Adopt a wait-and-see attitude. It's possible you'll learn something.

A more complete discussion of discipline comes at the end of this chapter.

Some Rules for Babysitting

While every family and every situation are different, here are some basic rules when you babysit.

1. Before the parents leave, be sure that they tell their children that you are in charge. One time our usually well-behaved younger son was exceptionally disobedient to a visiting grandmother who babysat for the evening. When questioned the next morning he said, "She doesn't live here, so I didn't know she was the boss." Make sure that your grandchildren know who's the boss.

Parents should transfer this authority to the grandparent in the presence of a child so there are no doubts. Details of activities while the parent is away should be clearly given. Let it be understood that when the parents return, they will ask the grandparent how things went—and a grandparent *always* tells the truth.

2. Be a bit more strict at the start—then you can ease up. If you're too lax at the beginning of your babysitting session, it's sometimes difficult to gain control later.

3. Let grandchildren show you how things are done—where they eat, how they play after supper, the bedtime routine. Even if you know these things already, let them take the lead. Go along with their ideas as much as possible. This doesn't mean that the teenager is allowed to hang out at the corner market until 10:00 P.M.

4. Have some special activity planned. Now that you have your grandchildren all to yourself, use the time wisely. In advance, think of a game, a sport, or a craft that can make the babysitting time go speedily and smoothly. You'll feel your hours spent were more than just caretaker time. You'll actually be giving something special and making the time valuable.

With young children, it's a good idea for a parent to produce a box of toys that the child hasn't played with recently. This can make the babysitting time interesting for the children, since they'll look forward to the contents of the box that has been kept out of reach on a high shelf.

5. Give older youngsters their own space. Don't be with them, talking to them, guiding them every minute. Bring along your own reading and projects to help fill the time. But be very available for talk. As with younger children, encourage a joint activity if the youngster is interested.

6. Don't let TV take over. Look at the TV listings with the youngster and select one or maybe two shows to look at together.

Perhaps the parents will have let you know the names of approved shows. Following the viewing, turn the TV off and go on to other activities.

7. Be consistent and firm when you correct. Use words the child understands. Make it very clear what is right and what is wrong. Don't let a child wear you down. If you give in, you may lose control and could have more trouble the next time.

8. Be very calm, be ready to laugh, and don't take offense. Ignore unimportant infractions of the rules. Sometimes kids are just testing you with their antics.

9. Find the middle ground between strictness and spoiling the child. Some grandparents spoil their grandkids, thinking that shows how much they love them. Forget that idea. Kids respect order and they like parameters, so let them know just how far they can go. Don't permit junk foods, long phone calls, sloppy habits, or continuous television viewing or video game playing. Have fun within the framework of the family rules.

10. Mean what you say. Mean it the first time. Don't give second and third chances. That wastes time and dilutes your effectiveness.

11. Don't make threats you can't follow through on. If you say, "We won't go for a walk until the toys are picked up," don't change your rule. Be insistent and consistent.

12. Use the word "No." It is short and to the point. Don't beat around the bush with children. When you must say "No," be ready with a "Yes." "No, you can't jump off the roof, but yes, you can jump from this tree branch." "No, you can't go to visit the guys, but yes, they are welcome to come here."

Helpful Hints from Grandparents

The grandparents in my survey have logged a lot of hours babysitting. Collectively, they have watched over two thousand grandchildren. That's a lot of experience!

Most all of them babysit for short periods of time, but some sit daily for working parents. About half have taken kids for a vacation away from their parents. While babysitting once a month was most common, it's unfortunate to note that about 20 percent of nearby grandparents never babysit at all. These were mostly widowed grandfathers—perhaps this is just a sexist tradition that women are better caregivers. Or perhaps the grandfather felt unqualified or ineffective. However, in many cases it was merely his indifference and his choice. Of course, this is both his loss and, more important, his grandchildren's loss.

Many of the grandparents who spend time with their grandchildren admit that they enjoy the time more when the parents are not present. They say they are more "themselves" and have more fun because they feel they are totally in charge and not being observed, and possibly even criticized, by the parents.

One grandmother insists on one-on-one time and calls it "buddytime," not babysitting. This is a good term because as the youngsters get older, they no longer want to be referred to as babies.

"Let's make a deal" is a grandmother's method of getting compliance. She says it's not bribery, but a lesson in learning the art of accommodation and compromise. When her grandson is stubborn, she creates a deal: "You turn off the TV, and I'll show you how to do a trick." "Please clean up the kitchen, then we'll go for a walk." She says this system works for all ages.

Earning "Brownie points" is a grandfather's idea. For each instance of willing help, kindness, special cooperation, or obedience, he assigns a number that he dubs "Brownie points." These can then be traded in for a later bedtime or some special treat.

Going to the library is a feature of one grandmother's babysitting. While the kids are finding their books, she's finding some for herself. When they get home, they see who can find the most unique place to read: in the bathtub, in a tree, with the dog, under a table, even on an exercise bike.

One pair of grandparents prefers to watch over the young people at the grandparents' house. The grandmother has the saying, "My house, my rules" and this lets her make some special disciplinary points. She can say, "I know you don't wear a shirt to dinner or ask to be excused at your house, but this is my house, my rules." She also has the line "There are many acceptable ways of behavior, so do it your way at your home, but here. . . . "

Another grandparent carries the rules idea a little further. She has made up a simple list of do's and don'ts for her grandchildren's visits to her home or when she babysits at theirs. She goes over the rules early in the visit and reports she has no problems. In fact, the parents have incorporated many of these rules into their own family rules.

Pick your fights! That's what one grandfather says. He recommends that you think twice before you correct a child. If it isn't important he merely says, "Oh really?" and lets it go. But if it is important, he says, "Oh yeah?" and takes a firm stand.

Homework supervision can be a hassle. The grandparent is usually at a disadvantage not knowing the work that has come before or the exact assignment for the present. One grandmother uses this method: She asks her two grandchildren to explain assignments to her as if she were a student. This helps the youngsters to carefully verbalize what must be done. She then asks them if it is a fifteen-, thirty-, or sixty-minute project. She checks on them every fifteen minutes and celebrates with them when it is satisfactorily completed on or ahead of schedule.

There's a saying that one grandparent has perpetuated. She says "*This* Grandma has *standards*!" She has said it often at those times when the grandchildren have tried to put one over on her. Now they do what they're told and in a kidding way say, "I know, I know, Grandma has standards."

One grandmother goes to her daughter's home each time a new grandbaby is born. She serves as nurse and cook, but most important she lets the mother rest while she gets the baby on a good schedule. She recommends this book that she uses—and leaves with the family: *My First 300 Babies* (Hendricks, Vision House, 1983).

Another grandmother knows the importance of helping an older child adjust to a new baby. She becomes the special friend of the older child, reminding him of his own abilities and privileges. She's also good at explaining the great amount of time and effort that goes into baby care and how he can help. Her input does much to alleviate jealousy and allay fears.

Two grandparents always bring along a bag when they babysit. It's called "The Good Guys Grab-bag." It doesn't contain presents; it contains messages on three-by-five-inch cards. When a child has been good, he can pull out one card and enjoy the message, which might read "Let's make popcorn" or "Everyone has to do a trick for you" or "Stay up five minutes later."

Have Times Changed?

Today's youngsters will be the first to tell you that life is very different nowadays, so discipline should also be different. They'd like to sell you on the idea "If it feels good, it must be okay." Not true! Improper behavior still demands correction.

The goals of parenting remain the same. Even the environment in which the family functions is not so different from twenty years back. Don't believe that kids "can't help" doing the wrong thing because of peer pressure or world problems. That's just an excuse that compounds the problem.

A generation ago there were temptations, wars, fads, and corruption—that's an unfortunate thread through history. It is still the duty of parents to guide their children through these challenges. The biggest change—and one for the better—is in our responses to behavioral problems. We are seeing the necessity of helping kids *value* good habits, rather than blindly accepting (or ignoring) rules.

But even if today's discipline is somewhat less physical and more intelligent and gentle, we still want our children to raise our grandchildren to be responsible, educated, and caring young adults. These were also desired traits a generation ago. In research for my book *Working Parent—Happy Child* (Abingdon Press, 1990), I found that the old-fashioned traits are still endorsed by parents.

The order had changed slightly over the years, but these were still what parents most wanted their children to embody. I've listed them in order of importance to present-day parents.

1. Self-esteem
2. Love
3. Intelligence, creativity, inquisitiveness
4. Self-government, orderliness
5. Responsibility, poise, leadership
6. Honesty, ethics, religious faith, patriotism
7. Ability to communicate
8. Cheerfulness

If we ourselves made mistakes and raised our children, for example, in an extremely authoritarian way, or perhaps in the highly permissive method that was popular in the 1960s and 1970s, we may find some of our mistakes coming back to haunt us via our grandchildren. However, many parents who came out of those extremes are finding a workable middle ground. They may call it "new discipline," but in many ways, it is the same style used by thinking parents of past generations. We'll consider some of these methods in a moment.

When Do Grandparents Discipline?

If you aren't going to put in your two cents worth of advice each time you visit the kids, *when* do you provide input? Grandparents in my survey cited several important times when they had to be in charge and establish good discipline.

1. When a grandparent is the day-care provider. With the increasing number of working parents, many grandparents are called upon to contribute considerable hours of day-care for grandchildren.

Studies have shown that youngsters who spend more than twenty-five hours weekly in day-care respond to the discipline methods used by the care-giver. So, it is confusing if the parent—in the evening and on weekends—adopts a very different form of discipline.

Here there is a need for communication and coordination so that the grandparents and parents have similar aims. In discipline, consistency is basic.

2. When a grandparent is totally in charge for an extended period of time. This could be as an unofficial guardian (for example, when you are taking a youngster on a long trip) or when you are made legally responsible for the welfare of the child.

This situation sets aside the parent's methods in favor of what the grandparent feels will be right. Of course, the parent's previous training is taken into consideration, but the grandparent is now responsible and must do what he or she sees as best for the child's development. When the grandparent is in charge to this extent, he *must* have the authority to discipline in the way he feels is most effective under the circumstances, even if it is very different from methods formerly used by the parent.

3. When a grandparent is dealing with step-grandchildren who have suffered from a confusing number of authority figures. In step-parenting, the subject of disciplinary methods is one of the most disruptive and divisive. Often, for the benefit of the child, a grandparent is asked to be a mediator. This third party can sometimes sort out the emotions of both the broken relationship and the new family relationships. Then the grandparent can help set up a workable plan for harmonious living.

4. When babysitting. This, of course, is the most common time for grandparents to discipline. When parents trust their parents to care for the children, there needs to be an understanding as to what the parents want. But there also should be the understanding that the grandparent is free to occasionally try other acceptable methods. This should not confuse a child and it may result in ideas for better discipline by the parents.

In these normal babysitting times, a grandparent should know the family rules regarding what foods can be eaten (and where and when), bedtimes and bedtime routines, where youngsters can play (outside, down the street), telephone use, TV viewing, homework, chores, and so forth.

It's very important, when a grandparent spends many hours as the disciplinary/authority figure, that there also be other occasions of togetherness with the grandchildren—ones that are informal and unstructured. During these, the parent is the disciplinarian, and the grandparent returns to the normal role of supportive friend.

The Importance of Dialogue

The grandparents in my survey listed discipline as the most serious parenting problem for their children and the major point of disagreement between grandparent and parent. Many grandparents feel that the parents are indecisive, apathetic, or, at the other extreme, too harsh or physical in their methods.

When you are going to be in charge of your grandchildren for a period of time, you need to know what discipline methods the parents are using. You should follow these methods unless there is good cause to do something different. A good rule to remember is never say yes if a parent has said no.

Coming into a situation, a grandparent may not realize the parents' current aims. Some grandparents have the tendency to correct everything a child does wrong. Grandparents are often so knowledgeable that they fall into the habit of guiding or teaching every minute. (This can make for a major amount of tension in the child.) The best disciplinary program focuses on only one or two areas at a time. The others are temporarily ignored.

For example, the parents may be working on toilet training the baby or personal responsibility in the grade-schooler. These are the areas they have deemed most vital. So a grandparent/babysitter should also focus on these aims. Thus neat table manners and a perfectly written book report may have to take a back seat for now.

It can be hard for a grandparent to keep quiet on other problems or infractions. But knowing that a child functions best when being guided in just a few areas at one time, you may want to make a "Things-Jeremy-should-learn-someday" list for yourself. Just getting the problems written down will make you feel better. You can bring up these subjects with the parents at a later time to see how your ideas fit in to their parenting plans.

Asking parents what their current goals are, taking up problems with the parents first, supporting the parent's current aims—these can help maintain a good relationship within the family. And it still provides you with the opportunity to help your grandchildren in specific social and emotional ways.

Is Grandpa More Fun?

During the question period at one of my grandparenting seminars, a confused grandmother asked me: "How come our grandchildren think I'm terribly strict, but grandpa is just a sweetie-pie?"

While the question seems humorous, it is a serious topic. In their dealings with grandchildren, far too many grandfathers prefer to let the grandmother take the authoritarian role and they just follow along for the fun. Consequently, grandchildren think that the grandfather is the soft touch—the easy-going, happy guy.

Because women often outlive men, grandchildren are exposed to far more grandmothers than grandfathers. Thus, when there are grandfathers on the scene, they need to take a very essential role in the lives of their grandchildren. Youngsters need to see full lives, as well as commitments and interest, from both grandmothers and grandfathers.

Since many years may have passed since dealing with babies, many grandpas defer to the grandmas when a grandchild is an infant. It can become difficult for the grandfather to enter into the relationship as the child gets older. It is at this point that many adopt the "good guy" approach and hold back from making any meaningful contribution to the child's life.

As in other aspects of living, equality is needed here. Both grandparents should have opportunities to lead and follow, correct and instruct, and laugh and be serious. Don't allow yourself to be typecast as the ogre or the "sweetie-pie."

Modern Methods of Correction

Although the grandparents in my survey said they didn't like to discipline, they still agreed they had to have a method when caring for a disobedient child. Almost all of them said they first tried friendly persuasion. Then, when that didn't work, they took other steps. It escalated to, as one said, "the swat/slap/spank level."

Such physical methods of correction are inadvisable for several reasons. First, they teach children that an adult (and thus appropriate) way to solve a problem is with physical force. Unfortunately, kids are quick to adopt that method and soon they are hitting their playmates in order to get their way. Also, when kids are spanked or slapped, they remember the humiliation and hurt, but tend to forget the problem that the adult was trying to correct. Spanking makes a child resentful of authority, and hence less teachable.

If our aim is to show a child a better way to act, we need to select other methods when persuasion fails.

For young children, "time out" is effective. This means that a child is removed from play or other activity and put in a quiet place to think about what she did wrong. I like to use a low bench that I call "The Thinking Bench." The adult either stays with the child or sets a timer for the length of time the child must sit quietly and think. After a while, adult and child talk about alternate ways of acting. Then the child returns to play, very aware that the misbehavior has taken away precious play time.

Another effective method with young children is an expression of great displeasure or unhappiness from the grandparent. The child is surprised and impressed that something he has done has caused the grandparent sadness or hurt feelings. Because he, too, has experienced unhappy feelings, he will be less apt to inflict them on others by repeating the mistake. It is natural for a young child to want to please. In using this method, you must not be silly, but serious about your displeasure. Sometimes a bit of acting is required.

Often, a mere diversion to a different activity will solve the problem. Taking a child away from the source of over-stimulation, excitement, tension, or jealousy is sufficient. It also teaches a child to recognize impending trouble and step back.

With older children, deprivation is usually very effective. If a youngster does something wrong, she is deprived of a privilege. This is often the way it is in the world: If one breaks the speed law, the driver is fined and may lose his driving license.

This method works very well, provided you know your grandchild well enough to deprive her of something she really values. Don't be like the grandmother who told a disobedient gradeschooler that he couldn't go out and play with his friends. He didn't care—he didn't have any friends in the neighborhood.

The aim is to deprive a child of something he truly wants to do. For example, wrong action can result in loss of TV privileges, an earlier curfew, no telephone or car use, or the removal of a special toy, game, or video game.

The object of any discipline is to get the child's attention and encourage a better way to behave. You want to show the child acceptable ways to act under difficult or trying circumstances at play or school. Keep this foremost in mind when you correct a child. Discipline is not merely "Don't do that," but more importantly, "This is a better way!"

Being an authority figure in the lives of your grandchildren may not always be easy. Just remember what a grandparent told me: "It's nice to know that when we've finished babysitting, we get to go home to peace and quiet!" Well, enjoy the togetherness while you can. All too soon, the grandchildren will be grown up.

GRANDPARENTS' WORKSHOP

Being in charge of grandchildren is a great responsibility. One aspect of that responsibility is making sure the youngsters are safe.

Next time you babysit, take this quiz along and see how safety-conscious the family is. Some questions apply only to certain age groups of youngsters, so ignore those that aren't pertinent to your family.

Some of these are subjects that you can actually practice with your grandchildren (for example, question #2). Others are things that you can check on or recommend to the parents (for example, question #1).

1. Is there a list of emergency numbers by the telephone? And another list if the house has a second floor?

2. Do even the young children know how to dial the emergency number (911 in many areas), give their name and address, and stay on the phone to follow directions?

3. Do the kids know at least two ways to escape from each room of the house in case of a fire? Is there a meeting place (a tree or light post) where the family can rally and check that everyone is out of the house?

4. When there are toddlers, are all electric outlets carefully plugged and cords tied up? While you're looking at cords, check for frayed ones.

5. In case a child is cut, do all children know how to care for a wound and apply a bandage? Is there a handy first-aid kit in the kitchen or bathroom?

6. Can you demonstrate the Heimlich Hug—the method of bringing up food caught in the throat? (A kindergartner saved the life of a choking playmate using this method, so consider teaching it to the family.)

7. Are harmful objects such as plastic bags, knives, cleaning substances, and medicines kept safely out of reach of young children?

8. If there are guns in the house, are they always under lock and key? Do the grandchildren know to *never, never* play with loaded or unloaded guns or even show them to friends? Is the key kept where kids can't locate it?

9. Does the family have a system for answering the phone that protects a child who may be home alone?

10. Does the family have a system for answering the door that lets a child know who is there before opening the door?

11. If there is a swimming pool or other body of water nearby, is there a life-preserver handy? And does the child know how to use it? Is the hazard fenced?

12. When going out into the neighborhood, do the kids know the importance of going in pairs at night? And do they know they should never speak to strangers or go near to strangers in parked cars?

While the right response to these questions may seem obvious to you, you may be surprised at how little your grandchildren know. Since you love them, see that they know the answers and have these skills.

Eight

THE EIGHTH COMMANDMENT:

You shall encourage your grandchildren to be responsible members of a strong family

NOTE: Please do not skip reading this chapter just because your family is strong and loving. Granted, this is not a chapter about fun and games with the grandkids. But it contains important information for every adult—grandparent or not. It is an appeal for caring adults to join together in solving the problems of the disintegrating family. If you love your grandchildren—and want the best for their children and grandchildren—please read on.

Dear Grandma,

Our two daughters are married, each for the second time. Megan and Michelle are trying to be good mothers, and their new husbands seem sincere, too, although they all are very busy with their jobs.

Of our seven grandchildren, which include two step-grandchildren, only one speaks respectfully to his parents. The kids are noisy, messy, come and go as they please, and don't help around the house. And to top it all, one teenager is now pregnant.

The way the families live, I sometimes feel our daughters are in the hotel business rather than the home business. This is especially hard for me, since I live with one of the families and have to observe all this.

I'm a healthy sixtysomething and I feel I could contribute to the well-being of these families if I knew how to go about it. What makes a family strong these days?

MUDDLED MOM

You have every right to be muddled when you see family values disintegrating before your very eyes. The hard question is what you can do about it.

While your work as parent is over, you can't just stand back and let the family fall apart. Although it is much easier to keep a family strong from the start, it's certainly possible to put it back together.

Whether you actually live with a family or observe it from near or far, there are things you can do to encourage responsibility and caring.

Today, many of the ills of the world are squarely placed on the disintegration of the family and family values. But this didn't happen overnight. Although it has become desperately apparent in this generation, it began subtly years ago. Thus, we all must take responsibility—and take action to correct the problem. Just because it crept up on us slowly, we ought not to feel that it will also go away at the same snail's pace. We should work for, and expect, progress.

Why Get Involved?

Isn't this a problem that should be settled between parent and child? Hardly! The disintegration of the family has reached such magnitude that some people think it is a Humpty-Dumpty situation where "all the king's horses and all the king's men" can't put it back together again.

It will take the joint efforts of families, educators, religious leaders, and government authorities. Innovative programs and strict standards will speed progress. But the inevitable catalyst to make it all happen is the individual.

Grandparents who are on the scene can play an important part. Those who are far from their grandchildren can contribute to the welfare of families in their own home area. This can indirectly help solve their own family's problems by contributing to the general solution. Many grandparents have quite a bit of free time and are able to participate in part-time programs at youth centers and other social organizations. Their expertise and talents *can* make a difference.

Who Says It's a Problem?

Unless you have been asleep or can't read, the message is coming through loud and clear. What society calls "family values" have been ignored far too long. The results of diminution of family values have been carefully researched by various sociologists, child development specialists, and government agencies.

One of the most inclusive studies was compiled by the Office of Educational Research and Improvement of the U. S. Department of Education. It is called *Youth Indicators 1988, Trends in the Well-Being of American Youth*. It draws together, in one book, research from other government agencies, university scholars, and family-oriented institutes. It is not all bad news. There is hope. But *our* help is sorely needed. We all should care enough to take part in finding solutions.

The statistics in this chapter are from this report, unless otherwise indicated.

Where Did We Go Wrong?

Several generations ago, society deemed that family life needed improvements. The authoritarian and stern father and the compliant and uneducated mother were no longer the models for parents. Being a submissive child and starting to work early in life was thought unenlightened. Rather than looking deeper and taking the best from the old-time close-knit family and improving on it, most everything was tossed out.

Wars and depressions and more wars and good times came. We gave ourselves and our children whatever our hearts desired. Priorities got out of balance. Selfishness set in. The mottos were cute, but telling: "The Me Generation," "If it feels good, do it," "Why wait, tomorrow we could be nuked," "Let yourself go."

Without intending to, we taught our youth these faulty lessons:

1. The most important thing is money. Get as much of it as you can, as fast as you can.
2. Love is sex. Extramarital sex doesn't hurt anyone if no one knows about it. Forget the word *abstinence*.
3. Try marriage by living together first. That way there will be fewer divorces and less pain if you split.
4. Television viewing equals leisure. After a day of work, the best thing for you to do is to pig out on fast foods and trashy television.
5. Kids are smart, and they'll turn out okay if you just leave them alone. Correcting them could stifle their growth and individuality.
6. If you don't feel good about your life, there is a drug that will fix things for you.
7. Everyone cheats. Try not to get caught.
8. There is no Supreme Being. And, if there is, who needs Him?
9. You deserve to have what you want now. After all, things could be worse tomorrow.
10. Let the other guy look out for himself.

Although thoughtful people want the very opposite of these statements to be true, you might have a hard time convincing many grandparents, parents, and youngsters of the merits of even hoping for something different. They've been conditioned by repetition and experience.

Thus, in our deluded way, we have created a world where two parents must work to put bread on the table. Stay-at-home mothers (or fathers) are denigrated. Children are raised by a variety of "others."

Premarital sex and marital infidelity, and the accompanying stress, heartbreak, pains, and diseases, are commonplace. We have unmarried couples with babies, single parents trying to go it alone, and kids with several sets of parents and step-parents. Nobody appears to be in charge.

Our favorite pastime is playing couch potato. We've forgotten the joys of many sports, games, and arts and crafts.

Kids smoke, drink alcohol, and do drugs—some as early as grade school. Many can't read well or hold a job. They cheat and sometimes steal, but don't feel it's wrong since they see adults (and even our elected officials) doing it, too.

Ethics and religion are considered old-fashioned and irrelevant to real life as it is lived today. Sunday? That's the day to sleep in. Forget what religion teaches about caring for one another. It's important to have it all *right now*. To heck with others; let them take care of themselves.

It is easier to state the faultiness of this kind of thinking rather than to make a positive rebuttal. But here are some very simple and basic arguments to refute the ten points numbered above:

1. Money has uses. But more important than what you earn is what you *do*. Who's looking after the future of your family while you're accumulating all that money? Money itself doesn't bring contentment.

2. Love is much more than sex. Guilt, sadness, and hurt can come from confusing love and sex. Each has a place and a time. Commitment brings great satisfaction.

3. Learn to like and respect yourself first. Then you are ready to be part of a couple and to respect another person. Couples who live together first and then marry are statistically more apt to divorce.

4. Avoid being just an observer of life (and avoid obesity at the same time) by turning off the TV. Have other interesting after-work activities that can truly refresh you and make you a more interesting person.

5. Kids benefit from good role models, creative educators, and adult guidance with firm standards and consistent discipline. What a child becomes as an adult is the result of input during the growing-up years. Remember the computer term "GIGO"—it means "garbage in, garbage out." What are kids "taking in" these days?

6. Drugs only temporarily blot out some personal misery. Drug users have four choices: to be cured, to go insane, to go to prison, or to die early. Take your choice, face up to the problem, and get control of your life.

7. Everyone does not cheat. Cheaters perpetuate that lie to make themselves feel better. Being honest will add to your self-esteem and success.

8. Yes, there is a God who has a plan for each of us. Many of the most distinguished scientists and doctors say there is "someone in charge of the universe." This knowledge takes a lot of pressure off us; since we know we aren't doing it all alone, we have the best help available, a loving, supreme parent: God.

9. There is pleasure in anticipation, in waiting for or earning something. Instant gratification becomes an impossible way of life, an obsession. Tomorrow can be (and so often is) even better than today.

10. We need one another. This need isn't just for company or doing good deeds, but because being with others makes our own life better, too. If we all abandoned one another to live on our own private islands, we would all soon die. We need one another physically, mentally, and socially.

What Are the Facts?

Census figures and reports of other research organizations and pollsters were combined in the *Youth Indicators* report to show the picture of a fair cross-section of today's young people. Here are some facts:

* *Alcohol/drug use.* Over 90 percent of high school seniors have used illicit drugs; over 65 percent use them on a monthly basis. The most used is alcohol, followed by marijuana and cocaine. Drug use reached a high (pun intended) in 1981, and took a slight downturn during the rest of that decade.

It is too soon to congratulate ourselves on any real progress here, as the drug situation is still volatile. Strict parental standards (prevention) and encouraging youngsters to seek help early (cure) are still the best answers.

* *Leading youth killers.* In youths aged fifteen through nineteen, motor vehicle accidents (which are often caused by intoxication or drugs) is the leading cause of death. Suicide is second. Homicide is third. The latter two are also drug related in many cases.

Statistics show a clear relationship between these youth killers and academics. Students who get good grades and/or are active in sports are less apt to be involved in fatal accidents. Suicide often stems from lack of self-esteem. Fortunately, these senseless deaths of children and youths are on the decrease.

* *Victims of violent crime.* Males are much more likely to be victims than females. Robbery, assault, and rape are all on the increase.

The statistics show that an increasing number of victims are gang members and innocent by-standers. Where there is neighborhood solidarity and caring (which combats gang solidarity), there is less crime.

* *School completion.* Here's some good news. Drop-outs are no longer on the increase; however, about 14 percent still do not complete high school. More good news: The number of youths finishing four years or more of college is soaring.

Failing to complete a high school education is the leading cause of joblessness. The gap is widening between the educated and the undereducated. While the educated are getting more education and bigger incomes, the undereducated are dropping into deeper poverty and homelessness.

* *School behavior.* Sixty-seven percent of school teachers say that disruption in the classroom is the same or has increased over a five-year period. School policies to combat this disorder are limited, because state laws are weak and ineffective.

Many teachers say that they are teaching less and disciplining more. They wish parents would send their children to school rested, fed, and ready to learn—and ready to respect the teacher.

* *Activities.* Weekday leisure activities of high school seniors have remained about the same in a decade—with television viewing way ahead of everything else, followed by reading books and magazines, and then getting together with friends. Sports is next. Work around the house, playing a musical instrument, singing, or working on a craft are way down the list.

The fact that parents are not at home is partially responsible for the high number of after-school TV viewers. Many youngsters lack direction in choosing positive activities for their free time.

* *Homework and television.* In a study by the National Assessment of Educational Progress, fourth-, eighth-, and eleventh-grade students were tracked as to the amount of time spent on homework and watching television each day. For fourth graders, 43 percent did less than one hour of homework, as compared to three to five hours of television viewing daily. Thirty percent look at six hours or more of TV each day!

Eighth graders were doing a bit more homework (57 percent were doing up to two hours), but 50 percent were also managing three to five hours of TV daily.

Eleventh graders (53 percent) were doing up to two hours of homework with 37 percent watching three-to-five hours of TV daily.

With the imbalance between studies and television, we can see that TV is having a greater impact on the minds of many young people than classroom training. The combination of television and homework—both sedentary activities—has made a generation of unfit children. An increased percentage of youngsters are overweight, and recent tests show a marked drop in the fitness of grade- and high-schoolers. This is combined with a trend away from physical activity and group activity in the after-school hours.

* *Unmarried mothers.* Births to unmarried women between the ages of fifteen and twenty-four are highest for black women, but that figure is gradually decreasing. While currently much lower for white women, this figure is on the increase. Births to unmarried teens have tripled since 1950.

Early motherhood usually means that the mother doesn't complete her education and thus has poor job opportunities. In general, these "children of children" in turn have much more difficult lives—poor role models, lack of education, less stable home life, and higher drug use. Thus the cycle often repeats itself.

* *Single parents.* The percentage of children living in single-parent families is on the increase. In 1985, 21 percent of all children lived in single-parent families compared to only 10 percent in 1965. More than one-half of all black children lived in single-parent homes in 1985.

Single parenting usually means that the children do not have guidance in the after-school hours. It is still too soon to know for sure, but early research on latch-key children indicates that they are less proficient in school and have greater problems with the law than youngsters with adult supervision.

* *Working mothers.* The labor force participation rate of married women with children under six years of age has been rising steadily since 1970. From that year to 1987, it rose from 20 percent to 57 percent and is continuing upward.

The pre-school years are the most formative for a child. Lack of parental bonding, increased aggression, and hyperactivity are some of the problems of children placed in day-care at a very early age. (From studies in 1985 by the University of North Carolina and Jay Belsky, a University of Pennsylvania psychologist. While some studies have refuted this, it is still too early to call.)

The pressure on women to hold down three jobs (career, homemaking, parenting) is beginning to take its toll health-wise. Male/female statistics on mental and physical health are growing closer together as women have increased job pressures. More available quality day-care, more support from spouses, plus work-at-home opportunities are only a few of the answers.

* *Divorce.* The number of divorces rose 15 percent annually between 1975 and 1985, following a 116 percent increase the previous decade. In the past few years, the number of children affected by divorces topped 1.1 million *each year*!

While causes for divorce can not always be nailed down, it is known that arguments over child-rearing and money are usually at the top of the list. Children who live in a pre-divorce and post-divorce environment often have emotional problems that affect social adjustment and educational achievement.

* *Money.* While median family income has remained rather constant, the spending ability of children has greatly increased. In 1985, about 42 percent of high school seniors had jobs and spent most of their earnings on themselves (clothing, records, recreation). Blacks contributed more of their earnings to meet family expenses than did whites. High school seniors planning to attend four-year colleges were more likely to save for their education than were other seniors who planned to go to a trade school or junior college.

Students relying on an allowance from parents have been forced to appeal for regular increases in order to keep up with buying needs. Saving for future needs is almost impossible—or considered unimportant—until about age twenty-six.

Young adults spend almost one-half of their food budget on food eaten away from home—an expensive practice.

* *Religion.* While 35 percent of high school seniors attend religious services weekly, about 50 percent attend rarely or never. Youth attendance has been declining each year in the past decade. However, almost 60 percent say that religion is important in life.

Other surveys show that when parents attend services, youngsters are more apt to follow suit.

* *Values.* High school graduates rated what they felt was

important to achieve in life. The answers were hopeful: (1) a happy home life, (2) a steady job, (3) sufficient funds for extras. However, each time the survey is taken, more money (number 3) inches upward. Correcting social inequalities (high on the list in the 1960s and early 1970s) is now in last place.

This rating of values is slightly better news than many of the other categories. At the same time, there is an increase in agreement between high school seniors and their parents as to what is important in life. It's a good sign when parents and children have similar ideals.

* *The place of grandparents.* In a survey of college students, Gregory Kennedy of Central Missouri State University found that these young adults see their grandparents as a stabilizing factor during times of family trouble. Grandparents were especially important to grandchildren in single-parent households. He also found that the students felt closer to their mothers' parents than to their fathers' parents. They also tended to be closer to grandmothers than to grandfathers.

Here, then, is substantiation of the vital link between today's youth and their grandparents. This is a door of opportunity for bringing back good family values.

So What Can a Grandparent Do?

These statistics represent children in general. These may or may not mirror your grandchildren, but these facts affect the kids in the neighborhood, your grandchildren's friends at school and in activities, and many of the young people working in service jobs who touch your own life. The young people represented by these statistics are real people who cannot be ignored.

As caring grandparents, we need to work harder to help overcome these problems for our grandchildren and for all children. We need to get involved.

In my own survey, grandparents cited what they felt were the biggest problems for their grandchildren. They felt that the biggest problem for younger children was a lack of consistent discipline on the part of the parents. Next was the amount of TV these children were permitted to see.

For older grandchildren, the grandparents' main concerns were keeping children free from alcohol and drug use. Following closely behind were concerns about the prevalence of premarital sex, about the lack of self-motivation, and finally about the young people's tastes in clothing, cosmetics, hair styles, and music.

For children of all ages, grandparents observed problems because of lack of respect for the parent, for other figures in authority (teachers, youth leaders, police), and for grandparents and senior citizens.

Grandparents need to make a time commitment to do their part in strengthening the family. If a grandparent gave a half-day a week, we could see in just a few years a marked change for the better in the statistics shared in this chapter. And grandparents could personally witness substantial changes in their own family.

Are you willing to take part in this important youth crusade? The hope of the children of the future is at stake. Why not make a commitment now?

GRANDPARENTS' WORKSHOP

What concrete things can you do to help strengthen the family?

Here are some vital ways grandparents can take action. Some are only possible for those living near the grandchildren, but some are possible for those living far away or making occasional visits.

Put a check mark in front of the ones you plan to follow up on.

1. Educate yourself about drugs and alcohol. Don't bury your head in the ground. Go to the library and borrow this book: *It's OK to Say No to Drugs* (Alan Garner, St Martin's, 1987). Send for free material from National Clearinghouse for Alcohol and Drug Information, P.O. Box 2345, Rockville, Maryland, 20852. Or you may call (301) 468-2600 for immediate information. When you are informed, initiate a series of suppertime conversations when grandchildren and their parents are present. Don't be heavy handed or accusative. Ask them to help you understand the peer pressure and the underlying basic problems.

2. Provide young people with some useful work they can do for you. This has many benefits. You get a needed job done at a reasonable price. The youngster earns some money. And best of all, you can help establish good work habits and get in some good conversation at the same time. Typical jobs are window washing, putting up storm windows or screens, yard maintenance, car washing, spring house cleaning, carpet cleaning, painting, repairs, and simple building projects. Success in completing a work project builds self-esteem.

3. Be a volunteer for a youth group. Consider what you can teach or share. Or perhaps you can chaperon, chauffeur, or cook. Also consider much-needed leadership positions in groups such as Camp Fire and Scouts. Check with your church, "Y," or Boys or Girls Club. Some jobs even provide modest pay.

4. Investigate foster parenting. If you have the time and energy to give, you can set a young life on the right track. You'll earn money for this, but your biggest pay will be personal satisfaction. This doesn't have to be a life-long arrangement. Most communities need short-term foster parents, too. If your time is limited, consider "adoption" of a child through one of the children's aid programs—you pay about a dollar a day and have contact through letters.

5. Ask if you can babysit a few times a month, even if the parents have other sitters. This will give you opportunities to get to know your grandchildren well. If your grandchildren aren't nearby, offer your services to parents in your own area.

6. Join the group called Action for Children's Television (ACT). This educational evaluation group will provide plenty of information on the good and the bad in television. You can actually have an impact on network show selection, and you can pass on your new knowledge to your grandchildren. The address is ACT, 20 University Road, Cambridge, MA 02138.

7. Offer to write some family rules for your grandchildren. Start by asking parents and children what rules are important to them or what problem areas need rules. Ask what they think fair punishments would be for various rule infractions. Combine all these ideas, possibly along with some of your own, into "The Family Rules." Next, discuss and finalize them in a way understandable to all. Type the rules and give a copy to each family member.

Then step back completely from the situation. In about three months, get together to assess successes and failures. Make needed revisions of the rules. Written rules are especially useful for grade- and high-school youngsters, since they provide a framework in which youngsters can comfortably move. Yes, they *do* like to know what is expected of them and what will happen if they disobey the rules.

8. Be supportive of the parents. After all, these are the children you so wonderfully raised. Reinforce the good ideas they have. Be gentle and non-critical in making suggestions for improvement (and do make suggestions, but never in front of their children). Regularly ask, "What can I do to help with the family?"

9. Speak up for good traits. Don't be afraid to talk about honesty, morality, respect, and responsibility—even with toddlers. Help youngsters learn how to disagree and how to express strong feelings about an issue without being rude and disrespectful.

10. Be there when you're needed. Be sensitive to the problems of the family, whether the problems are minor or major ones. An outside "listening ear" can help a child find her way through difficult times.

11. Have a "what if" discussion concerning suicide. Openly talk about the options a youngster has when he is depressed. Be aware of counseling agencies that can help. Encourage your grandchildren not to be ashamed to ask for help. Emphasize the importance and value of each child, no matter what his or her present circumstances.

12. Don't harp on mistakes, bringing them up over and over again. If a child has failed a class, smashed a car, used drugs, or gotten pregnant, she's been through hard times. Don't be sympathetic with the action, but be sympathetic with the youngster. Help her to find the way. Love her, no matter what.

How many of these ideas have you already utilized? How many more can you do?

Nine

You shall not judge your children or your grandchildren, but work together to solve problems

Dear Grandma,

What's the young generation coming to? They look weird, talk weird, act weird—and listen to music I can't understand. One of our granddaughters married a fellow of a very different religion. And one of our grandsons is dating a woman of another race!

We're a very close-knit family and we enjoyed birthdays and holidays together as the youngsters were growing up. Now that they're dating and marrying, I just can't imagine what our family get-togethers are going to be like.

OLD-FASHIONED NANNA

What are your get-togethers going to be? Fun! How exciting not to have a family of clones. Different doesn't mean bad or boring.

Different can be good and revitalizing. Your multi-faceted family is like a microcosm of the world—if *you* can't get along, how can the people of the world?

I know it takes a mental shift to appreciate other styles of living. Sometimes it is hard to understand why young people do certain things and choose certain friends. But remember, judging others isn't your job. Your work is to be supportive of your grandchildren and gently encourage the best in them.

When you judge, you put yourself on a pedestal and say, "I know what is right; you do not." That antagonizes others and cuts off communication. Outward appearances can be deceiving—what looks right or wrong to us may not be so. Of course, you might see certain pitfalls ahead, so without being judgmental you try to steer young people through the problem areas. Experience is a great teacher, and sometimes a youngster learns life-benefitting lessons from hard experiences.

So, let's calmly consider those things that rile us up the most. Grandparents in my survey were happy to list them. *The list includes everything from thumb-sucking and video game addiction to guys with earrings and babies born outside of marriage.* Perhaps the gripes that you have about your grandchildren are described here.

Thumb Sucking and "Blankies"

Let's start with the easy gripes. Pediatricians and child psychologists vary in their opinions of "kiddie krutches." One year, research will show that babies and toddlers who nurse, eat well, and are held and loved more, are less apt to require pacifiers, beloved thumbs, and tattered blankets. The next year, research will show that tooth decay and mal-alignment of teeth result from objects constantly in the mouth. But the next year, a different researcher will tell that these supports build self-esteem!

So stay out of it. Refer the parents to their parenting books or their doctors for current advice. Sometimes, you can distract a fussy baby so you won't have to look at a pacifier dangling from the babe's mouth. However, in most cases, reminding a child to take his thumb out of his mouth doesn't help one bit. He may oblige once, but it's usually no permanent solution.

There is one thing that you can do if you can't bear to see a grandchild walking about with a disreputable rag of a blanket clutched near her mouth. (Some parents give the lame excuse that they can't get the "blankie" away long enough to wash it. Doesn't the child sleep? Have they thought of just taking it away for an hour—after all, who is in charge?) Here's a solution: Cut an old blanket into four pieces. Hem them if you wish. Be sure they all look alike. You can sew a small rag doll into each one if you want. When a child is still a baby, let one of the little blankets be with him, perhaps around a doll or animal. Put another in the playpen or stroller. Put another around his bedtime toy. This way he will become comfortable with all of them. (And you'll feel better that the little blankets have some useful purpose, too.) Suggest that the parent switch them around, and wash them as needed. With several look-alike "blankies," one can always be in the wash or in for repairs.

Now, let's move ahead to more important gripes.

Learning Disabilities

Simple stuttering, dyslexia, hyperactivity, Down syndrome— whether the problem is small or large, curable or possibly not, we all must be supportive of parents with learning-disabled children, as well as with the children themselves. For many of these young people, the road to a satisfying life is going to be rough and they'll need all the bolstering they can get.

Certainly there are problems that just go away on their own. Many go away faster if we don't harp on them. But other problems require extraordinary alertness by the parents: watchful and patient home care, the giving of medication and therapy, and special education in school.

Here are some of the more obvious problems that you may need to be aware of as a grandparent. They are not covered in any depth here since personal professional assessment is needed. But they are problems that grandparents should be knowledgeable about.

 * *Stuttering* is not an uncommon problem among children learning to speak. It is usually caused by blocks or spasms interrupting the rhythms of speech. Being patient with the child and calmly listening to her without prompting will help. Don't suggest words or correct. Make communication as easy as possible for her. If it continues, contact a speech therapist.

 * *Left-handedness.* While babies are ambidextrous to about age two, one boy in ten (and fewer girls) will ultimately be left-handers. Don't pressure them to change since the hemisphere of the brain that controls handedness also controls language, and interference could result in later speech problems. Instead, help them with left-handed eating, drawing, and play. Buy them left-handed scissors. Be sure the parents tell the day-care and play-school teacher that a child is left-handed.

 * *Mirror writing.* This appears in various degrees of intensity. Some children write all letters backwards, some just the letters with ascenders and descenders (like b, d, g, or p). While it often cures itself, special instruction can also correct it.

 * *Dyslexia.* This term covers various reading disorders associated with the inability to interpret spatial relationships or to integrate audio or visual information. Few dyslexic children are mentally retarded in a way that will affect their ultimate abilities, but parents should be made aware of the problem so that special training is utilized during the early learning years.

 * *Down syndrome.* This genetic defect often results in mental retardation and weak muscle tone. This is a serious problem that requires special attention and much parental support and understanding. Some recent break-throughs are making life longer and more meaningful for these loving children.

 * *Hyperactivity.* This exaggerated physical activity is sometimes associated with neurological or psychological causes. Some of the recommended treatment methods are now under close scrutiny. Encourage parents to be very careful about medication given to control this.

* *Drug babies.* What mothers use during pregnancy—from coffee and tobacco to hard drugs—can result in great physical damage to the fetus. Research is just now being reported on the first group of teens who were born to addicted mothers. Learning and behavioral problems (poor attention span, aggressiveness, brain damage) don't often show up until school age, when these problems can make education and socialization extremely difficult. Educating young people as to the importance of avoiding these substances during pregnancy is imperative. You may want to lovingly point out this important topic to your children and grandchildren.

Youth Obsessions

While not as critical as learning disabilities, some of the obsessions of young people warp their social progress in very serious ways. Here again, your job is to be aware of the problem and be supportive about correcting it. Merely making critical remarks won't make a change for the better.

Most of these activities are acceptable, but problems arise when the time they consume gets out of balance. When this happens, other important activities that round-out a child's growing years get lost. We want our grandchildren to have the fullest lives possible. Permitting one activity to become all-consuming is a mistake.

* *Obsessive television viewing.* Start by having other activities available when grandchildren visit you. Don't let TV take over visiting time. Chapters 4 and 5 in this book will give you plenty of ideas of alternate things to do. Keep a list of things you want to do when the grandkids are around—and do them.

If the obsessive viewing is a problem at the child's home, you may want to talk to the parents about it. Sometimes parents are too busy to think of alternatives. It is *so* easy after a full day to just turn on the set and relax. The benefits of television, its risks, and means of controlling viewing are explained in detail in my book *Working Parent—Happy Child* (Nashville: Abingdon Press, 1990).

Judiciously choosing certain quality television programs will result in better grades, balanced views of sex, less aggressive behavior, and a wider range of interests.

* *Video game obsessions.* Because of a deluge of complaints from parents and doctors, video game companies such as Nintendo are trying to clean up their acts. Now there are finally a few games not based on violence, and there are a few that appeal to girls. But the main appeal is still to boys ages nine through fifteen. It is not uncommon for boys to spend one hundred dollars a month on new games and five hours a day playing them. Proponents say that the games improve mental skills and physical dexterity. But parents report an increase in negative behaviors such as aggression, lying, tension, and sullenness. Child psychologists label them as frustrating and stress-building for kids. When a child loses, he may react with anger, being upset over his inability to score higher and higher. One psychologist says that this obsessive need to score higher is akin to the chemically dependent person's obsession with "scoring" by using greater amounts of the addictive substance.

If you are asked to buy video games for a grandchild, choose ones that don't have scoring or killing as the main components. Read the game rules and strategy before putting down your money.

Encourage parents to limit game time at home. Again, as with television, there have to be alternate activities.

* *Music obsessions.* Many kids think that only one kind of music has any value: hard rock. Watching music videos and listening to recordings are their favorite activities. Certainly there are some good ones. But the messages of many of them are so downright disgusting that you wonder how those recording them can be considered "artists." These records blatantly encourage and glorify torture, killing, rape, extra-marital sex, and drug use.

Parents who can't deal with problems prefer to remain ignorant. Not wanting to know what is going on, they don't even bother to listen to recordings. They feel that if they disapprove, they have no means of coping with the problem. Buy this book as a gift for the parents: *Raising PG Kids in an X-Rated Society* by Tipper Gore (Nashville: Abingdon Press, 1987). Borrow it and read it yourself.

If your grandchildren ask you to buy them a cassette, say "yes," but that you'd like it to be in good taste and you want to hear it as soon as it is purchased. If they say "never mind," then you know you can assume you were being taken advantage of.

Remember, there's a lot of good modern music out there. Ask kids to share it with you and be willing to listen to it. Tell them of your own special musical interests. Mealtime is a good time to have music in the background, so encourage grandchildren to bring their recordings to your house.

Of course, the *volume* at which music is played is a great gripe of many parents and grandparents. Doctors are outraged with the amount of hearing loss that this generation of kids is suffering. Some municipalities are beginning to take action with laws regulating the volume of the music that spews from vehicles. But, since more music is played at home, this won't do much good until parents make a few laws there.

Try not to lump all youth music together and judge it as evil. Be modern and search out some pieces that you like. On the other hand, don't sit idly by and accept as "part of growing up" the evils of lyrics that degrade. Young people appreciate good protesters, so make this one of your causes.

* *Obsession with clothes, hair, and cosmetics.* Here we confront a dual obsession. Kids are obsessed with what they wear and how they look. Grandparents in my survey were obsessed with their disdain for mod clothes, exotic hairstyles, and elaborate makeup.

When youngsters go out of their way to look very different from their elders, they're usually trying to establish their own individualities. Sometimes they go overboard; sometimes peer pressure forces them to make selections they wouldn't choose on their own. Don't let these outward appearances distract you from appreciating the inner child.

One grandmother took photos of her uniquely dressed grandchildren. A year later, when she shared the photos with them, she noticed that they poked fun at some of their own clothing. I had a similar experience. One of our sons, looking back at a picture of himself with shoulder-length hair, said, "Why didn't you tell me to get it cut?" I'm sure we must have suggested it, but we felt that hair, makeup, and clothes do not "make the man"—or the woman.

If you judge by outward appearance, and most of us do on our first impression, you may not like what you are seeing. But a leather jacket, heavy eye makeup, or frizzed hair isn't the end of the world. Kids will grow out of it and all too soon they're in a world that requires more conformity. So if clothes are clean and not indecent, why not let your grandkids enjoy them for a while?

The cost of conforming to youth fads is often a big one. Clothes are not cheap, but if you encourage the parents to establish a clothing budget for each gradeschool-aged child and older, kids will learn to make choices and get their money's worth.

In some school districts parents have joined together to stop clothes competition. While private schools have long had school uniforms or outfits, many public schools are seeing the economy of uniform or similar clothing. It certainly puts wearing apparel in perspective and lets kids get on with learning.

But if modern youth fashions really bother you, you can try some of the following:

1. Go shopping with your grandchild. See all the unique clothes for sale. Be encouraging about ones you like—or can tolerate. You may even want to buy part of an outfit.

2. Find out when a store is giving free facial make-overs. Invite your granddaughter to go with you. Let the professionals redo each of you. You'll both learn something new and useful, and the "dragon lady look" may give way to better makeup.

3. Comment very favorably on a grandchild's appearance when he wears something more acceptable to you. He may wear this again in your presence.

4. When going out in public with grandchildren, announce the dress code to both your adult children (the parents) and the grandchildren. Be specific. You may not always win, but at least you tried.

5. Suggest this idea: At one end of a youngster's closet, parent and child put a couple of "acceptable" outfits—jacket and shirt that go together, jeans that aren't in tatters, clean slacks and shirt, and so forth. Call it "the parent's corner." When wearing apparel matters to a parent, all he has to do is ask that something be worn from "the parent's corner."

6. For a birthday or other gift occasion, offer to buy an outfit, with the understanding that it has to meet your approval as well as theirs. This is not as hard as it sounds, and it can be fun shopping together.

* *Obsession with cigarettes, alcohol, or other addictive substances.* While some of this has been discussed already in chapter 8, these undesirable habits must not be condoned by grandparents. Some adults think it is "cute" to include young people in the drinking of wine, beer, or other alcoholic drinks. It is hard to discourage young people from these habits when they see their role models smoking and drinking. Presently, preteen girls are the biggest group starting to smoke. Treat these habits seriously, as life-threatening. Don't be passive here. These obsessions/addictions are not "grown up" any more than is putting a gun to your head.

Religion and Politics

These two topics are family powder kegs as kids become more mature. It's easy to approve of people who think and act as we do. We're comfortable with folks who have the same activities, join the same groups, choose careers we like, and spend their leisure time in ways similar to us. But you will find that as your grandchildren get older, there may be a divergence in life-styles, especially in beliefs concerning religion and politics.

Keep calm. One grandparent says, "I don't even mention those two topics!" That may avert strife, but it also averts discussion. If you can keep your cool, why not talk? Both sides can be enlightened. It isn't necessary to declare a winner. Who's to say what's right? Just be grateful your grandchildren are intelligent and informed enough to have an opinion. If their discussion doesn't include good facts, it may be apparent that they're getting swept along with the crowd.

Concerning politics, we're all becoming much less party-oriented and are more concerned with how the candidates stand on issues. You'll find your talks on this subject go much better if you focus on the issues and not on the person.

When we began dating seriously, my husband and I decided it was time to get our parents together. They had many business and social things in common and we thought they'd hit it off. Somehow the first topic to come up led to a discussion of political figures. Speaking of an election some years before, my father said he'd have voted for Mickey Mouse before he would have voted for Franklin Delano Roosevelt. It was an electric moment when my husband's father said almost simultaneously that FDR was one of the world's greatest men. Yes, they let us marry, but we never let them talk politics again.

Within our own family, we have a wide range of political interests. When our daughter was in high school, she decided to work in support of a candidate. Although neither we nor the grandparents supported that candidate, we were all very proud of her interest in issues and the "white papers" on various subjects. We let her know that we admired her work. It was a good education for all of us in the family to have a close-up view of one aspect of politicking.

If you disapprove of your grandchildren's politics, remember that life is long. As young people mature, their ideas solidify or change. Encourage them to vote and be grateful when they do. Different political beliefs aren't worth a schism in the family.

If politics can make the emotions run high, you can imagine how differences in religion affect the family. For many of the growing-up years, children usually go along peacefully accepting the same beliefs of their parents and grandparents. Then may come subtle comments, and finally an explosion. One day you realize that your grandchild doesn't have the same religious beliefs that you have.

At first this may take the form of a youngster protesting: "I don't want to go to church." But if religious observances have been a "given" since childhood, this may not happen. Sometimes association with a church youth group cements a child to her religion. Or perhaps grandparents can attend as well, and the protesting might cease.

Actually, the most effective method for encouraging youngsters to be interested in the family religion is for the adults to live their religion, day by day, showing it to be practical both physically and emotionally. That is the certainly the best commercial!

But often the time comes when a child decides on another religion or leaves religion behind entirely. When this happens, we feel that we, too, have been abandoned. On one hand, we encourage kids who think for themselves; on the other hand, we feel sad when they do.

Take heart. A large majority of kids who have had childhood religious training and then opt out of that church return at a later date—quite often in their thirties. This usually happens because they feel the need for social friends, or they have a personal spiritual need, or they want religious training for their own children.

Some youngsters leave because they find another church more satisfying. With religions growing closer together in theology, should it really bug you if your child is an Episcopalian or a Presbyterian? It's usually your pride that is damaged. Instead, be glad that the young person values church enough to investigate and make a choice. It's doubtful that God recognizes different denominations. The important thing is to have faith in a Supreme Being and live a moral life. While we might like the grandkids in the religion we've chosen, we have to remember that it is their life, their choice.

Don't be snobbish about the choice. Visit the new church with your grandchild. Without sounding like The Inquisitor, find out what attracted him and how it differs from your religion. Be pleased to have a grandchild who values religious principles and is willing to take time for church attendance.

A harder situation is where two young people who plan to marry come from different religions and neither wants to forsake his or her teachings. After money and children, a main cause of marital disharmony is difference in religious outlook. Certainly it is more enjoyable to attend services together, but many marriages have survived with the participants attending different churches. This is most difficult when there are children involved. One Sunday here, another Sunday there doesn't make for a real feeling of "church home," and as they grow up, children with this background are apt to choose nothing.

Often the best solution is for this couple to find and join a middle-ground church, one that offers some of the traditions and teachings of each of their own former churches. A family unit needs shared experiences. Weekend religious observance is one more tie that binds.

Encourage your grandchildren to take part in their church activities. If you live nearby, be willing to be chauffeur or chaperon. If you live far away, don't hesitate to talk about how your religion has made your life better. By making church a part of life, we keep the teachings alive and growing. When we are hesitant to talk about religion, we give the impression that it is just an old habit and doesn't really matter.

But, whatever your grandchildren decide, it isn't up to you to be the judge. Remember the words of Malachi: "Have we not all one father? hath not one God created us?" (Mal. 2:10 KJV).

Love and Marriage

One day you hear that your grandchild has fallen in love. Sometimes this love is followed by an engagement and marriage. Sometimes it is followed by falling out of love, sometimes by a living-together arrangement. And sometimes it is followed by a baby born out of wedlock. What do you do now?

When you don't approve of your grandson's beloved, it is easy to complain and say it is the parent's fault—or the school's or the church's. Maybe there wasn't fault at all. Maybe this young man just found a sympathetic, attractive person who thinks he's the tops!

So what if that young woman your grandson wants to marry has been married before? Or that young man your granddaughter wants to marry wears an earring? Is it time to go into shock, to throw up your hands, to assume the world is coming to an end? For many grandparents, these decisions are the hardest to think through. Inwardly we hoped for our youngsters to enjoy love and marriage as we knew it, or at least fantasized about it. When they don't choose what we wanted for them, we act like spoiled children.

If you keep close to your grandchildren during their young adult years, you may have an opportunity to know their friends and lovers. Perhaps you'll find them agreeable when you get to know them. But you may find them quite disagreeable. Tell yourself this: "I love my granddaughter. She loves this man. If she sees things in him to love, I can too." Then do it.

Of course, the situation of young people living together before marriage is so common today that we hardly take note of it anymore. But when it happens to your precious grandson, you really sit up and take notice. How could he do this? Can't he make up his mind? How can I explain this to my friends? What will everyone think?

Actually, you aren't responsible for your grandson, so you don't need to explain it to anyone. It's none of their business unless you make it your business and theirs. No doubt your grandson already knows your feelings about couples living together.

One grandmother punishes a granddaughter who is in a long-term live-together arrangement. She almost pretends the young man doesn't exist. She gives gifts to the granddaughter and not to her live-in. She tells the granddaughter what she *would* give if they were married. This is certainly a form of tyranny and grandchild abuse. How much better to be supportive of the things she does like about her granddaughter's friend, and hope and pray for a legalized arrangement later!

There can be many reasons why young people choose not to marry. They may be invalid reasons in your eyes, but this isn't your business. Your business is to love them.

Then comes that nightmare moment when your grandson Brian confides in you that he and his beloved Laura are going to make you a great-grandparent. But, they can't (or won't) marry. For many grandparents, this announcement can be the low spot in the three-generation relationship. But all is not lost.

Certainly we would prefer that Brian and Laura marry. But if that isn't possible, don't cross them off your list in anger and disappointment. Don't judge them harshly. At the right time, suggest a "Commitment Service."

Let's say that Laura's divorce won't become final until after the baby is born. In the meantime, Brian and Laura will be living together as if they were husband and wife. All the relatives are aware of what is happening, and there is a general buzz in the family. At this point, the family needs to join together in support of the concept of family.

Yes, it is sad that there can be no legal or religious service yet, no coming together to support the vital concept of marriage. But a Commitment Service can bring harmony to the situation. This is not a fancy party with gifts and friends; that is reserved for those who marry. This is a quiet but happy time for just the family members to meet in a supportive way.

The service really isn't a service, it's just a simple get-together in a living room or in a private outdoor location. A parent may open the gathering by thanking the others for coming. Each of the others has brought something to share: a poem, a thought, a Bible verse, some kindly advice, a helpful hint. The prospective parents can pledge their love to each other and the unborn child. Perhaps the group will want to repeat a passage together, such as The Lord's Prayer or the verses on love from chapter 13 of I Corinthians. Maybe the group could form a circle and hold hands for a quiet moment at the conclusion of the sharing time.

Sometimes refreshments or a simple meal will follow. It is nice when a photo is taken to commemorate the event. Or perhaps everyone will sign their names in a small guest book. While it in no way takes the place of a proper marriage service at a later date, the young adults, parents, and grandparents who have held Commitment Services say that they feel much better afterwards.

One grandmother shared an especially touching story of her daughter's marriage. She told how sorrowful she and her husband first felt when their collegiate daughter fell in love with a young man of a different race. But they were wise enough to recognize the importance of supporting their daughter's decision to marry.

They now have grandchildren who are of a mixed heritage, and they happily observe that both parents are active in teaching their children patience, obedience, love, kindness, and acceptance. The grandmother says she loves them so much that she doesn't even *see* the difference in color anymore. She has found that love is colorblind. She notes how talented and helpful these youngsters are, and how much the three generations enjoy being together despite the differences in background. Respect and caring are not the private property of one race. She and her husband love these children and they are loved in return. What more could a grandparent ask?

Yes, grandchildren can "dress weird"; be forgetful, messy, or rude; or have an obsession. Maybe you think they're making some big mistakes. (Haven't you made a few yourself?) Decide what is really important in the overall picture of your grandchild's development. Be quick to forgive and forget. Don't carry grudges. Have no hurt feelings. Permit no estrangements. Keep the channels open no matter what. Don't let judging get in the way of loving.

GRANDPARENTS' WORKSHOP

Do the manners of your grandchildren cause you embarrassment? Do you often feel critical of how they act at home and in public? If so, you can do something about it. Borrow from the library or buy a copy of an up-to-date etiquette book. *The New Manners for the 90's* by Letitia Baldridge (Rawson Associates, 1990) or *Miss Manners' Guide for the Turn-of-the-Millennium* by Judith Martin (Pharos, 1989) are two good choices.

Next time you are with your grandchildren, take along this quiz and see who can choose the correct answers. (Don't peek at the answers below.) You may want to look up other questions in the etiquette book, too.

1. When someone asks you a question and you have food in your mouth, you should:
    a. Raise one finger to indicate you'll answer shortly.
    b. Do your best to answer but keep one hand in front of your mouth in case you spit out food.
    c. Discreetly remove the food from your mouth and place it under a lettuce leaf on your plate.

2. On a date, the boy opens doors and holds chairs for the girl. She doesn't like this, so she should:
    a. Just go along with it and figure he's an old-fashioned guy.
    b. Tell him not to do those things since she isn't old or infirm.
    c. Wait until she knows him better and suggest that those niceties are unnecessary for her.

3. You're invited to a party and the invitation says RSVP. You aren't sure you want to go. Should you:
    a. Keep your options open by telling the party-giver you're a "maybe"?
    b. Accept and then not go, saying later that "something important came up"?
    c. Force yourself to make up your mind well in advance and tell the party-giver?

4. You are at a large informal dining table and someone asks you to pass the salad dressing. You want some too, so should you:
    a. Quickly serve yourself and then pass the dressing.
    b. Ask if you can have some on the way.
    c. Ask that they send it back to you when they've finished.

5. A group of your friends and some of their friends that you don't know stop at your house for a snack. Your mother comes in. Should you:
    a. Introduce those you know and not mention the others?
    b. Ask each one to introduce himself?
    c. Say, "This is my mom," and hope the others will tell their names?

6. Grandpa has filleted the fish, but you get a bone in a mouthful of fish. Should you:
    a. Lower your head to table level and carefully remove the mouthful into your hand?
    b. Leave the table, and spit it all out in the kitchen sink?
    c. Wait until someone else is talking, then remove the bone, placing it on the edge of the plate?

7. You are opening birthday gifts with the givers watching you. Grandma has given you a wallet you can use. Then you open cousin Lindsay's gift and find it is identical. If neither offers to exchange the gift, should you:
    a. Say: "You both have good taste. I'll use one now and save one for college"?
    b. Pretend you don't notice the duplication and go on to the next gift?
    c. Say: "Well, I have one to use and one to give as a gift"?

8. The holiday dinner is going on and on. At a break before dessert, you rest your lower arms on the table while talking. You have:
    a. Done something socially acceptable at this specific time in the meal.
    b. Broken the "no arms on the table" rule.
    c. Forgotten that arms on the table are always acceptable, but elbows never.

9. At a gathering of friends, the subject of an upcoming party is raised. You realize that not everyone present is invited. Should you:
   a. Offer to get the others invited?
   b. Try to hush up the person talking about the party?
   c. Say, "Oh yeah, let's talk about that later"?

10. Your grandparents have brought you a truly wonderful Christmas present that you thanked them for when you opened it. Should you:
   a. Thank them again when they leave?
   b. Mention it next time you're together?
   c. Write them an appreciative note?

Answers:
1. a; 2. c; 3. c; 4. b; 5. b; 6. c; 7. a; 8. a; 9. c; 10. a, b, and c

Ten

THE TENTH COMMANDMENT:

You shall love each of your grandchildren no-matter-what

Dear Grandma,

We know that our years of child-rearing and correcting are over. And we really love our grandchildren, even though they do some things we don't approve of. Nevertheless, we want these youngsters to feel the deep love and concern we have for each of them. For those grandchildren nearby, it's easy. For those far away it's more difficult. What are some ways we can show this love?

HUGGABLE GRANDPARENTS

Wanting to show love is the vital first step. We have a great start if we don't feel uncomfortable or embarrassed about kissing and hugging. And we have to put aside the fear of being rebuffed when we're affectionate.

Many people find it difficult to say the words "I love you." Sometimes this comes from having said those words to someone we no longer love or someone who no longer loves us. We've been hurt, and we don't want to be hurt again. Perhaps we have been brought up in a family that didn't openly express love. Or maybe we have made the mistake of thinking that love indicates approval. We think we can only love those who are lovable.

But love imposes no conditions. It isn't "I love you . . . *if* you do what I say," or "*if* you live a life-style I approve of," or "*if* you are good to me."

Love has no strings attached. It is love, no-matter-what. When our children were young, I always told them we loved them no-matter-what. Occasionally one would come to me and say: "You know how you always say you love me no-matter-what? Well . . . ." I always knew some sorry tale was about to be told!

Now with grandchildren, you have taken one step back from the day-to-day guidance. But you haven't taken a step back when it comes to giving love.

Love is ageless. We aren't too old to love or to be loved. And our grandchildren never outgrow the need to be loved. Certainly it is easiest to cuddle and love the new baby in the family. But what about the sweaty six-footer? He, too, needs your love.

Love has principle; it has backbone. There may be times when you know it is wrong to do something your grandchild wants. Because you know right from wrong, your love makes you say "no." That may not seem kind from the youngster's point of view, but your love requires you to respond in accord with your principles.

That's why we can't confuse love with permissiveness. Many grandparents do. Letting a child be undisciplined, selfish, or rude will hurt him in the future. Because we love him deeply, his bad behavior can't be condoned now, in the formative years. Remember that good parenting line: "I love you too much to let you do that."

Love knows no gender. For centuries we have associated affectionate behavior with women. Now we're correcting that mistake. The showing of love is a strong feeling, and can be masculine as well as feminine. Some grandfathers still defer to grandmothers in the hugs and kisses department, but grandfathers and grandsons can learn to talk and act lovingly. It just takes a little doing and a little determination not to be put off by a new-found emotion.

Your love-oriented actions—hugs and kisses—won't be brushed aside if you start when your grandchildren are babies. Then it's natural. It can stay natural. Make a welcome hug and a good-bye kiss traditional with you. Walk hand-in-hand when you go outside—not just when crossing the street. Make story-telling a time for lap-sitting closeness.

Some youngsters are harder to love than others. I know some wonderful grandparents whose granddaughter has mental retardation. They have found that a visible demonstration of love is the best medicine when she is disruptive. When her actions make her seem totally unlovable, they pour on the love, and she usually responds.

Wise grandparents use lines like these:

Because I love you, I have to say that what you are doing is wrong.
If I didn't care about you, I'd just give in.
I love it when you smile.
I'd love to help you pick up the mess.
I'd love to go along with what you want. I'll try it your way if you'll try it my way next.
I don't *like* what you're doing (or saying), but I always *love* you.
Your love means a lot to me.

That last line was written *to* a grandmother from a grandson in prison. Later, when he was released, he said that the unconditional love of his grandparents was one of the biggest factors in giving him the self-respect to make amends and start a better life.

A granddaughter was expelled from school by the principal over the strong objections of the classroom teacher. The grandfather talked to the child about the great lengths the teacher had gone to in order to help her. Concerning this teacher he said, "She must have tried very hard to show you she cared about what was happening to you. She must have loved you a lot to want you to be successful in her class." The gradeschooler thought a moment and said, "When I go back, I'm going to be so good that my teacher will be happy." One person's caring love *can* make a difference.

These no-matter-what examples of love in difficult circumstances make many of the other problems we might have with grandchildren seem small by comparison.

Signs of Love

Beyond hugs and kisses for all ages, you can create your own loving traditions.

A grandfather we know says that his arms are long enough to hug several grandkids at once. He always stoops to kid-level when the youngsters arrive and he sweeps them into his outstretched arms.

One grandmother shares her family's love tradition. At the end of a family get-together they form a circle and send the triple hand-squeeze message of "I love you" around the circle.

Another grandparent with a wheelchair-bound grandchild said that hugging isn't comfortable for the child, but he loves giving and receiving "High Fives" and blowing kisses.

A large grandpa and his equally large grandson like to give each other friendly whacks on the back when they greet each other. These days men are now exchanging more than a hearty handshake. Many give actual hugs, and kisses are even becoming more common.

While there are a few people who don't like to be touched in any way, you'll have good success if you start the hugs and kisses when kids are young and keep them going all through life. Keep these hands-on love signs frequent and casual. They're just one part of love.

Words of Love

Our family often uses the acronym RILY when we say good-bye or at the end of letters. It is our symbol for *Remember I Love You.*

We all *do* have to remember our love. Sometimes our language doesn't show it.

If we love people, we don't tear them down. We may correct them or disapprove of what they do, but we don't indulge in gossip or judging. Our words match our true feelings.

When talking with their children and grandchildren, grandparents can choose words that help—or words that hurt. Listen to these words that turn off the listener:

> Where did you get that outfit?
> Because I said so.
> But he has a beard!
> That's impossible.
> I hate that music.
> Shut up.
> You think you're so smart.
> You never do anything right.
> I never change my mind.
> I'll never forgive you.

When we're speaking to someone, there are many words and phrases that give a warm glow. How much better to use these lines:

> That's okay, you tried.
> I'm so glad you're my grandchild.
> What can I do to help?
> I have a surprise for you.
> I'll consider it.
> Let's fix it together.
> How nice you look!
> I miss you.
> No one else could have done it as well.
> I couldn't wait to hear your voice.
> I like just being with you.

Find opportunities to use these verbal hugs often. You might refer to this list just before your next family get-together.

Far-away grandparents can tell love stories on the phone, write loving letters, or make cassettes or videos as described in chapter 1.

How we talk about family and friends is so important to children. They are quick to pick up on our anger or prejudice or bitterness. Kids assume we're just as critical of them when they hear us verbally pick apart other folks. Mean and nasty talk puts everyone on edge, too.

But sharing words of kindness, compliments, and even constructive criticism with grandchildren can be very satisfying and can reinforce the youngsters' self-esteem. Sometimes we can show our love by just holding our tongues and being quiet.

We must be careful not to sound cold or unfeeling. That can happen when we're not sure what to say—as when a grandparent is no longer living. For example, if grandma has died, don't leave her out of conversation. It is a sign of love to share stories about her activities and her antics. It is a responsibility of the surviving grandparent to keep the memory of the deceased one alive. Silence gives the impression of gloom and finality, rather than joy and the hope for continuing existence.

Talk in private also shows affection. Huddling close, whispering, exchanging secrets—this kind of talk strengthens the bonds of love between the generations.

Deeds of Love

Kids learn by example. They are watching all the time. They take in experiences and process them, letting them be guidelines for their own actions. In addition to what you *say*, what you *do* as a grandparent is meaningful.

Have you ever thought of the unique link we have from generation to generation to generation? With other (non-human) forms of life, one generation teaches the next with actions and minimal sounds. But they have no way of benefiting from the experience of generations farther back in family history. A chimpanzee or a dolphin has no way of knowing what its "grandparents" thought or did.

Human beings can benefit from the experiences of many preceding generations. What an advantage we have! Let's not waste it. Whether you are a grandparent or great-grandparent, let your light shine.

Your good deeds are vital signposts in family history. The casserole you made for a grieving family, the welcome home flowers for the new mother, the spur-of-the-moment invitation for pizza and a movie, the card of welcome to a new neighbor—such simple deeds can show a caring love.

Sometimes the care that one grandparent gives to another is a powerful lesson. If, for example, the grandfather is very ill, the grandmother's devotion can show youngsters an enduring kind of love. When a grandparent is ill—even dying—don't deprive grandchildren of contact unless it is the strong wish of the sick grandparent. These brief times together can be very inspiring, and should a grandparent pass on, the grandchild will hold a feeling of having connected with a valiant person. Youth is resilient. Learning loving care within a family is a grand lesson.

My grandmother always wrote me on pale green stationery scented with English lavender. For many years I saved her letters describing her childhood in England. Perhaps that's why I was so pleased to find in my survey this story of a grandmother shared by her husband.

She, too, had some colored note paper—except hers was a powerful shade of pink. Although she didn't want to use it for her social correspondence, she thought her grandchildren might find it fun. Over the course of a year, she used an entire box of fifty sheets of paper and envelopes in writing to her two grandchildren. The notes weren't long, but expressed an interest in the grandchildren and also gave insights on her own life.

They looked for the bright pink envelopes in each incoming mail and loved getting the cheerful messages. They responded with letters and phone calls of their own. Getting a "pink note" was often a high point of their day and they saved them in a desk drawer. When the grandmother suddenly died, they found much comfort in the "pink notes" and later put them in boxes and eventually took them to their own homes so they'd always have these memories of a caring person.

Grandparents should be alert to ways they can encourage a grandchild to show love to his parents. The grandparent shouldn't take any credit for this, but just hope that such caring becomes a natural part of the child's nature. Sometimes kids want to show love, but just don't know how to go about it. Give them ideas and a behind-the-scenes push.

Sibling Rivalry and Family Friction

When three generations of a family can't get along, when certain family members are openly hostile to each other, or when youngsters constantly fight with siblings, added strain is put on all the family. Whether it is a sister-and-brother or a mother-in-law/daughter-in-law squabble, it spells t-r-o-u-b-l-e with a capital T. Let's consider these one at a time.

Competition between kids doesn't necessarily mean they hate each other. Sibling rivalry comes in many guises. It is a very strong emotion, but psychologists say that some rivalry is normal if it isn't a predominant character trait of the participants.

Some youngsters may feel that their siblings receive more love, so they vie with them for affection. Reason combined with love given over a period of time can reassure a youngster of equal treatment and affection. Some children express rivalry because they really enjoy competition and excelling. Others are looking for compliments and the reassurance that they are persons of value.

Whatever the causes, this sibling rivalry can be distressing—and parents and grandparents can't wait for kids to outgrow it. However, it starts with toddlers and often continues into the young adult years. If it is caused by low self-esteem, the answer is to give youngsters opportunities to succeed. (You can't *give* self-esteem to kids, but you can give them opportunities to accumulate self-esteem.)

Love and appreciation are the best medicines here, and grandparents should give liberal doses of each when they can provide it sincerely. Encouraging the individuality of each child helps, too. When a child is helped to understand that there are things that only he can do in this world, rivalry decreases and self-worth is enhanced.

When a new grandchild is born, be alert to give special loving care to the older sibling. This child may be thinking with anger or jealousy, "Wasn't I good enough? Why do I have to share things now? Why did they need another child?" This is where grandparents can come to the aid of parents in two ways: To reassure the older child of his own importance and individuality and to help the sibling to accept the new baby as an important part of the family.

When babysitting, you'll also decrease sibling rivalry if you don't make comparisons between the grandchildren. Avoid competitive games that pit one child against another. Don't grant special privileges to one sex (usually the female) or always place the blame on one sex (usually the male).

One grandmother who babysits often has what she calls the "Love Award." It is a pottery figure of a cuddly looking pooch that had been relegated to the back shelf of her storage closet. When she brought it out and showed it to the grandchildren, it was an immediate hit. Both children wanted it, so she placed it on their bathroom counter so both could enjoy it. However, when one child was excessively unloving to the other, it moved to the other child's dresser top. If both were mean, she took it home. While it didn't decrease competition, it did provide a reward for loving behavior.

Adults feel competition and rivalry, too. It's sad, but those mother-in-law jokes have some basis. A talented and very experienced mother-in-law is often compared with the new, talented but inexperienced young wife. That's not a fair fight!

When a grandparent has a new daughter-in-law, granddaughter-in-law, or when there is any new member added to the family such as a stepchild, your work is cut out for you. No doubt the new family member has heard glowing stories about you, or has been warned about your sharp wit or your great chocolate cake. Since you face a long-term relationship, start it off right by finding the newcomer's fields of interest or areas of excellence. As much as you'd like the newcomer to get to know *you*, play down your stunning achievements. Subtly point out the things that the newcomer has done or can do—things you aren't a pro in. Find a project you can do together. Be oh-so-easy to get along with. Be sure not to skewer others with your rapier-like tongue. The newcomer will fear that the way you talk about others in their absence is the way you'll talk about her, too. Wage a campaign to win over the new person with your intelligent kindness.

Sometimes it isn't easy when the newcomer strikes first. But that is usually the famous "good offense" that is deemed the best defense. Be slow to anger, slow to return a slight in kind. Uneasiness makes people do strange things. Give the newcomer every benefit of every doubt.

Try not to give helpful hints! Often a parent will give a message to a son that is really intended for the son's wife. ("She'd be prettier if she didn't wear so much mascara.") This not-too-subtle meddling will certainly get back to the wife. If you must say something, say it directly. Don't make your child be the middleman. It isn't kind—and it usually boomerangs.

You have had a couple of decades to get to know and love your own child. Now, that child has a spouse. Take a couple of decades of being kind and forgiving before you judge your child's mate. If you try to undermine the spouse, two things can happen: (1) your own child will dislike your actions and defend his spouse, or (2) you'll succeed in driving a wedge between the two and a family break-up could result. You don't need that on your conscience.

There *may* be some very unlovable daughters-in-law in this world, but your son found in this woman something to love. You can, too.

A word about private times between grandparent and adult child: Let's say that your son Barry has married Tiffany. Of course, you have many times with all of you together, and with the grandchildren. But, Barry is *still* your son, and it is natural for you to want occasional moments just with him. This is no slight on Tiffany. She'd probably love to have some private time with her own mother. You may have to ask for a lunch of just you two, or, happily, your very insightful daughter-in-law Tiffany may suggest it. What a gem she is!

When Grandkids Complain

The grandchildren in my survey were asked about how they got along with their grandparents. They were amazingly united in the answer to that question. They really loved their grandparents and loved being with them. But weren't there some things they didn't like about grandparents? Again, they were quite complimentary. But certain themes began to repeat and I thought it was interesting to know their major complaints (which are really quite minor).

In their own words:

"Telling me to pick up the toys, pick up the toys, pick up the toys. Gee, I'm not deaf."

"Going grocery shopping is really boring. They take so long and don't buy good stuff."

"Having to take a nap. I think they were the ones who wanted the nap."

"My chores had to be done *so* perfectly. It took me twice as long. I usually just whip through them."

"Going to visit old folks or hospitals. I didn't know what to do or what to say. But, I was better the second time, so I'll go again."

"Going for a drive. I don't think it's fun to just go for a drive. I like to go some place."

"When they talk as if I'm not there."

"Making little mistakes into big news and telling everybody about it."

"Saying they love me, but not acting like they do."

Now, those gripes weren't too bad, were they? But hidden in those statements are some interesting observations that we can all learn from.

Proxy Grandchildren

Sometimes circumstances mean that your contact with your own grandchildren is quite minimal. You can share your love by being a proxy grandparent and having proxy grandchildren.

When we lived in Hawaii, both sets of grandparents were far, far away. At church, however, we met a couple who were apart from their grandchildren living in the Midwest. We enjoyed one another's company immediately, and these PGPs (proxy grandparents) became part of our extended family. They babysat, shared birthdays and holidays, joined us at the movies or the school carnival, and exchanged little gifts. Now, many moves and many years later, these loving and lovable PGPs are still a part of our lives.

There are many children who would welcome a PGP. Look for your proxy grandchild at church, at a boys or girls club, or through friends or neighbors. Just because you aren't blood relatives doesn't mean you can't have the same special relationship you might have had with your own grandchildren. This cost-free love connection can bring much joy into both your lives.

A Love Story

I'd like to tell a true story about my mother and our older daughter. Grandma and granddaughter had a close bond right from the start and really enjoyed being together. We had to be out-of-town for Claire's first birthday and grandma had not only provided a suitable celebration, but also taught the party girl how to walk that day! In later years they shared private jokes and grandma even taught Claire some Swedish recipes and basic Ikebana flower arranging.

One time Claire was staying at grandma and grandpa's home for two days while we were having another baby. They lived in a woodsy area on a street that had a landscaped center traffic circle. The circle had about a thousand daffodil bulbs in it and the flowers were the pride and joy of the neighborhood each spring.

On this particular day, grandpa was off playing golf and grandma was in the laundry room ironing. Kindergartner Claire came and said, "Will you please stay in the laundry room until I ask you to come out?" Grandma agreed. After about fifteen minutes she returned with the same request. Minutes later, she announced that she'd be ready in just a while. Finally, when grandma was getting *very* curious, Claire came and announced: "Have I got a surprise for you!"

And did she ever. She hugged grandma, took her by the hand, and led her down the hall and then through the entire house. In every room there were daffodils—daffodils in pails, daffodils in pots, daffodils on each piano key, daffodils in the drinking glasses, daffodils with handmade hearts and poorly spelled and poorly lettered signs that said "I love you Grandma, hugs and kisses, Your Claire."

The one place there were not daffodils was the circle outside. Grandma smiled and laughed and cried, and they hugged each other. What a tribute! Of course, Grandma couldn't be angry—although I understand she later said to Claire a few things in a constructive way about community property. That afternoon, to make amends to the neighbors, they made fifteen daffodil bouquets and delivered one to every house on the street. So from a possible local revolution came a happy ending.

To love and to be loved—what more can a grandparent ask?

GRANDPARENTS' WORKSHOP

Consider how much you show your love to your grandchildren. If you have a spouse, include him or her in thinking about how you might improve this part of the grandparent/grandchild relationship. These questions will be springboards for some of the aspects of love you'll consider:

1. Do I tell my grandchild "I love you" at least once a week (in person, by phone, by mail)?
2. Am I comfortable giving my grandchild hands-on expressions of love, such as hugs and kisses?
3. Do I love my grandchildren equally, not favoring one over another?
4. Does my everyday language show how much I care for my grandchild?
5. When I must correct a grandchild, is my correction consistent but caring?
6. Do I talk with my grandchild about love—loving sisters or brothers, loving parents, loving neighbors, loving people who are different, loving other children in the world?
7. Do I tell my own children (the parents) that I love them just as much as when we all lived under the same roof?
8. Do I add to the circle of love in our family by including others, rather than excluding them because they are in-laws or step-relatives?
9. Do I let my spouse know how much I love him/her and what a precious privilege it is to be grandparents together?
10. Have I widened my circle of love by contributing my time and love to non-family members through church and community activities?

Love is one commodity that doesn't run out. You just can't use it up. As you share it, you multiply it—so spread it around!

Eleven

Grandma's Grab-bag

In preparation for writing this book, I sent questionnaires to many grandparents. Good ideas were shared by these folks from across the United States and Canada, as well as from England, Switzerland, and Australia. To their unique suggestions, I've added some of my own ideas that have been tried and proved worthy. In them, you may find just that special something for your next visit with your grandchildren.

Grandpa's Foreign Language

I tell my grandkids that there are some words that I don't like and some that are foreign because they have no meaning to me. These words are outlawed at our house. Along with the usual four-letter words, the outlawed list includes phrases such as "Shut up," "I hate . . . ," and "You're stupid." The grandchildren all cooperate! There's an added benefit—we have cleaned up our own language, and not just when the kids are around.

Combat Clothes

I'm a "hands-on" grandma, and I believe in getting right down on the floor for rough-and-tumble play or messy finger painting. Sweatsuit and sneakers make up my grandparenting costume. I bought three bright outfits on sale—ones I can just toss in the washer. My grandson knows we're going to have fun when he sees me in one of these outfits, which he calls "Grandma's Combat Clothes." One day we used fabric paint to decorate one of my shirts with a wonderful picture of a boy on a bike. Naturally, as the artists, we signed our work. So I now own a real original!

Cross-country Travel

Long car rides are way down on the popularity list for our grandchildren, but here's an idea that added fun to one cross-country trip we took with five of us in the car. We identified license plates and kept a list showing each state and its motto. We had an atlas along so we could learn the state capital. Then we shared facts about that state—things like location, products, bodies of water, and historic and tourist attractions. One day, our grandson kept seeing cars from one particular state. He said, "Let's not visit there—everyone has left to find a better place to be!" We eventually found license plates from forty states and eleven foreign countries.

Grandma Camp

That's what an overnight at my house is called. We cook meals outside and sing around the fire after supper. If the weather is good, we sleep under the stars. But if we sleep inside, we still use sleeping bags. We eat from mess kits I found at an army surplus store. After a morning of al fresco breakfast and outdoor games, we're ready for a change-of-pace and so we treat ourselves to an afternoon at the shopping mall!

So Little Time

When we know that our grandchildren will be with us, we plan activities that are enjoyable for them, but also constructive or educational. They live so far away and since we don't see them often, we want to have quality time with them. We choose events where we can chat and laugh together, avoiding movies or tours where you can't talk. At the end of each visit, we have an informal rating of what was best and worst. That's a helpful guide to us for when they visit again.

A Bird in the Bush

One of the greatest events for our grandchildren is joining us on the annual Audubon Society bird count. We usually take the two oldest children with us and they just love it. One prefers to be the secretary, writing down what birds we see and how many. The other likes to be a spotter as we tramp in the woods and across fields. Already the younger grandchildren are looking forward to the time when they can join with us in this event.

The Census and the Reunion

Our family gets together for a big country-style reunion every ten years, at the start of each decade. We remind everyone of the date years in advance and then months ahead so all can plan on being there. While the actual reunion takes just one day, many stay around longer and take side-trips, depending on their funds and distance from home. Everyone contributes food, games, stories, and jokes. And, of course, we take a picture of the whole crowd.

Essential to a good reunion is getting everyone to look forward to the date and to save the vacation time to be there.

Literary Gifts and Chats

Every year, we give each grandchild a magazine subscription as one of his gifts. But we've found that as they grow, their interests change, so we make it a point to talk with them about the magazine. We don't want to waste our money! We want the periodical to be one that the youngster is truly eager to read. One granddaughter is on her seventh different magazine subscription, but that's fine, since her changing interests make for good conversation with us.

Subject and Object

When three generations get together, this is a good game to play. One adult and one child leave the room and decide on a well-known character and an object associated with the character (such as Popeye and a can of spinach, or Mary and her little lamb, or President Lincoln and his beard). When they return to the room, they announce which of them is the character and which is the object. A timer is started, and everyone else is free to ask questions of the "subject" or "object" requiring yes or no answers. Usually the "subject" is guessed first, and the "object" quickly thereafter. Keep track of the time it takes to guess each pair. The pair with the highest score (the most minutes and seconds) wins.

The Secret Garden

Each year, one of our grandchildren gets to plant a garden at our house. It can be flowers, vegetables, or both. We go together to buy the seeds, then work together on soil preparation, planting, cultivating, weeding, and eventual harvesting. The youthful farmer comes once a week to tend and water the garden, although I may water it more often during hot weather. It's called "The Secret Garden" because each year we try one new type of seed and we don't tell anyone what it is until it is presented in a bouquet of flowers or a dish of salad or cooked vegetables. This is a great way to teach kids about gardening and also to get them to try new vegetables.

Who's Coming to Dinner?

At meals when there are three generations present, we have a special centerpiece. Using a spare picture frame, I place in the center of the dining table a photo of a relative—sometimes a childhood photo of a current family member, sometimes a photo of an ancestor. Everyone gets to look at the photo and tell who they think it is and what they think the person was like. This can get very humorous! After a while, I tell who it is. Then, we share the *real* facts about the person. Sometimes the person is even sitting at the table. It's a good way to get to know your relatives.

Grandma for a Day

Our grade-school grandchildren love to be "in charge." When they come to visit, we occasionally let one be the grandma or grandpa for the day. The one chosen sits at the head of the table, decides when we begin eating, what we'll talk of first, and reminds us of our manners. In the car, he sits in the front seat and directs the driver and even gets to choose one stop along the way. It's good practice in planning, navigating, and being kind to others.

Chairs and More Chairs

According to our granddaughter, our six dining chairs are magic chairs. She loves to line them up like a train and then ask me to be a passenger or the engineer or to sit way back in the caboose. Next, we turn the chairs into a horse and buggy, with two rows of seats. The chairs also have been made into a garbage truck, dentist's office, school bus, and fire engine. I get to play lots of different roles with my granddaughter directing the action.

In-law Labels

I don't like the term "in-law." I think of these chosen members of the family as "in-love" rather than "in-law." When referring to our four sons' wives, I just say "daughter." I know that confuses a few people and I sometimes have to explain, but I do think of these fine women as daughters—and they appreciate this distinction, too.

All Worn Out?

If the grandchildren tire you out, try my system that provides for periods of rest in an overly active day. Of course, the time together will probably include sports, games, and crafts. But sometimes I need a more quiet activity. So I wear a whistle around my neck. When I'm feeling tired, I just blow the whistle. This is a signal for the kids to stop what they're doing, race to the bookshelf, choose a book, and line up on the sofa. I then come and sit in the middle as storyteller. Sometimes, I let the kids who don't read tell the story by looking at the pictures. Often this story is better than the original. Either way, I get a restful break.

The Jewel Box

One rainy afternoon my seven-year-old granddaughter was visiting us. She arrived early and I hadn't finished dressing, so she was with me as I was putting on a pair of earrings. I could see she was very interested in the jumbled contents of my jewelry box. While I don't have any fabulous gems, she found each item quite enchanting. We took out every piece of jewelry and lined it up on the counter as I told her the names of certain stones, or stories about old pieces. She was thrilled when I gave her a little bracelet I no longer wear. We had fun together as we put everything back neatly.

A Changing Relationship

Because I have grandchildren ranging from toddlers to mature young marrieds, I'd like to comment on the changing relationship between grandparent and grandchild. When they are babies, I am an extra guardian, a nurse, and sometimes even a sage! Then, as they become older, I become a magician, a fountain of information, a straight-man for jokes, a willing accomplice in their games. Suddenly they are teens and I am a confidant, mentor, and sometimes a defender and advocate. Finally, when they are launched into adulthood, I'm considered the revered historian, and also something I've been all along—a very good friend.

Cloudy Sky, Dark Sky?

Our young grandsons don't mind a cloudy sky when they visit us. They know we'll bundle up in our jackets, go out on the patio, and stretch out on lawn chairs as if it were summer. What do we do? We look at the clouds and find faces in them. Sometimes we even name them and make up a story about the relationship of one face with another. (One might be a queen, another her poor but wise gardener, and so forth.) And, as the breezes blow, the faces change and we get to name them again or add to our story. Another "heavenly" activity of ours is going out at night and counting stars. Little ones just learning to count especially enjoy this.

Forgetful Grandpa

Our young grandkids live some distance away, so we see them only about once a month. When we first arrive, I pretend to be a forgetful grandpa. I say that I don't remember their names or where their room is. They like to take me by the hand and lead me to their room. Once there, I try to guess what is new or changed since my last visit. It's a good way to get the conversation going. Later, I hide something in the room and see how long it takes for them to find it. Yes, I sometimes "forget" where I hid it, but they usually find it by my next visit.

Grandparents' Day Gift

One of the nicest things we ever received on Grandparents' Day was a gift our children worked with our grandchildren to prepare for us. (We lived many miles apart at the time, so a big manila envelope was sent by mail.) Each grandchild had filled out a paper headed "Ten extraordinary, marvelous, wonderful, fabulous characteristics of Grandparents." On the reverse side it said: "A very special memory." We spent time reading and rereading the lists and the memories—and we felt so loved!

Mystery Table

I set up a card table in the middle of the living room when my grandchildren are coming to visit. They call this the "Mystery Table" because I make it different each visit. One time it will have a puzzle on it, and when nothing else is going on, we put some of the pieces in place. I give a prize for the one to put in the last piece. Other times I put a box game on the table for play later in the day. Sometimes I put paper and marking pens on the table and we draw names and make portraits of each other. Once I clipped cartoons out of newspapers, but left the captions off them. We had fun writing new and funny lines. Who knows what will turn up next on the "Mystery Table."

Pipe-Cleaner Man

My husband entertained our first granddaughter with a little figure he made out of a pipe cleaner. He called it Little Man. When he made the Little Man "talk," she was enthralled. He found that Little Man could say some things that a grandpa might not find easy to say. This granddaughter is now married and has asked if grandpa still has Little Man and if he would give it to her. When she becomes a parent, she'd like to have it so her husband can "do the talking" for Little Man and continue the tradition.

Race Grandma

Like most kids, our grandchild hates to pick up the toys at the end of the day. We've devised a method that makes it fun. Using a long piece of string, we divide the play area in half as fairly as possible. Then, he gets to choose which half is his to tidy and which is mine. When he says "Go," we start the pick-up-and-put-away routine. Once when we finished, he said "Let's bring out the toys again so we can put them away again!"

Kind Words

One of my favorite aspects of grandparenting is to compliment my grandchildren on something they have done or said, or how they look. Family life is so busy nowadays that sometimes the very essential kind words go unsaid. I try to find something to compliment each time we're together. Sometimes it isn't easy, but I look again (and sometimes again), and soon I find the needed kind words. I include our own children—the parents—in the compliments when I can. Everyone needs encouragement and appreciation!

Can We Do Lunch?

Now that our grandchildren are teens and enjoy eating out, I like to invite just one to lunch at a time. My husband does this, too. These one-on-one exchanges bring us closer to our grandchildren, who feel very special when they aren't treated as a group, but as interesting individuals. I don't make it a formal affair; sometimes I call on the spur-of-the-moment and ask, "Can we do lunch today?" One Saturday morning, a granddaughter responded, "You're exactly what I need since everything is going wrong." After an hour together I could see that she had a better and more hopeful perspective on the problems she was facing. When we lunched again a few weeks later, all was roses in her life.

Thanks for the Plank

At a building site, I saw a carpenter tossing a long and wide piece of wood into the refuse dumpster. I asked to have it and he was glad to have this warped wood taken away. It was just what I was looking for! This wide plank, which I elevate at one end with varying heights of wood blocks, has provided hours of fun for me and my grandchildren. We've done simple things like seeing who can make a marble roll the entire length without having it fall off. We've put marbles under numbered paper cups and had races. More recently, we've been using it as part of a speedway for race cars and trucks. One side we keep smooth, but we've put some curvy grooves on the other side to make our games more interesting. We sometimes practice "walking the plank" blindfolded. When the grandkids go home, it stores easily in the garage, ready for their next visit.

Wall Motto

I like to do calligraphy, so I lettered a little motto for the wall of each grandchild's room, centering each line so it looks like a pyramid. It says:

Read books.
Pray every day.
Respect Mom and Dad.
Take care of the things I have.
Be kind to my enemies—they need it.
Remember that Grandma and Grandpa love me.

Mobile Music

Facts: (1) Car travel can get boring. (2) Sometimes kids are too self-conscious to sing at home. I put these two facts together and came up with "Songs for the Road." Whether we are going to a movie with our grandchildren or on a long excursion trip, we sing along the way. (It's easy to sing in the car since no one is especially watching you.) I started out with some song sheets, but now we know most of the songs from memory. We do all the favorites like "I've Been Working on the Railroad," "Mule Train," and "Chattanooga Choo-Choo," and we try to learn one new song on each trip. We've even used some sing-along cassette tapes, but we really enjoy our own style and improvisation better.

I'm a Character

I'd like a nickel for every bedtime story I've read to my grandchildren! But, when it gets dull, I get inventive this way: I change the name of one of the characters in the book to the name of the grandchild. That's easy to do and makes the story more fun. Sometimes I name one of the characters or animals in the story for me. I don't mind being a cat or an elephant or even a talking dinosaur. In one story I pretended to be the gorilla. The next morning when I joined the family at breakfast, I stood by the table and swung my arms and pretended to scratch like a gorilla. We loved our private joke and my grandchild burst into laughter amid the amazed looks of the others.

Like Me?

When a mealtime needs a little lightening up, play the game "Why is it like me?" Near the end of the meal, one person leaves the table and the others decide on an object in the room (the salt and pepper shakers, the meat fat left on a plate, a rose design on the tablecloth). The guesser comes back and goes around the table asking each person, "Why is it like me?" The answers are often funny: "Because it shines," "Because it is fat," "Because it is valuable," "Because it disappears quickly," and so forth. Occasionally an answer may be a bit insulting, but this encourages everyone to have a sense of humor. The guessing goes on until the guesser identifies the object. The last one to give a clue is the next one to go out. We've adapted the game for restaurants, the guesser hiding his eyes as we point to the object.

Holidays Without Grandchildren

I've made it very clear to my children that I don't have to be with them and the grandchildren on every holiday. I realize they have other relatives, friends, and activities. I love being included, but when I'm not, I don't weep. Sometimes they call me in the morning to wish me "Happy Easter" or "Have a great holiday weekend." Long ago, I realized that if I'm going to be alone on a holiday, there are other grandparents in the same boat. I gather these friends (and some new acquaintances, too) and we have our own celebration. That way when I talk with the family later, I can ask what the children and grandchildren did that day, and I can share my event, too.

Cousin Closeness

When there are many grandchildren, there are often two about the same age, but from different families. We try to invite these two to our home at the same time, so that there are just two cousins and two grandparents. This provides the opportunity for them to get to know each other without siblings around. We've found that close friendships and camaraderie have resulted. And it's enjoyable to be a foursome for the day or overnight.

Treasures

Treasures are wonderful to share. I consider my grandchildren among my greatest treasures. Like worldly treasures, it is best when they are shared with others. While I love and value them, I don't want to hang on to them too tightly. I know they won't disappear. I want them to feel the freedom to be themselves and to know that I love them for their uniqueness. My treasure box is full to overflowing with many loving memories.

Twelve

The Last Word

Dear Grandma,

When I read articles or books on grandparenting, I get all fired up. But then after a few months of using some of the good ideas, my husband and I fall back into our old ways. By old ways I mean the same family chicken dinner every Sunday, bribing the little children with candy, criticizing the teenagers—well, you know, just being ordinary grandparents. Are we stuck in a rut or is there hope for us?

CHICKEN DINNER GRANDPARENTS

Any grandparent who provides chicken dinner every Sunday is wonderful! All you need to do is add some bells and whistles to the meal. You may want to review chapter 4 of this book for ideas on how to give the chicken dinner a new look.

As for falling back into old habits, we all do that occasionally. The old ways are *so* comfortable. But, if we don't want to be just mediocre grandparents, we need to make an effort to add flair to the activities we do with our children and our grandchildren. You need a master plan, a plan that will take you just one step at a time. You have many happy years ahead with your grandchildren. Actually it's a lifetime of happiness, so there's no reason to do it all at one time. Little-by-little is best.

First of all, you need to realize just how important you are to your children and grandchildren. You aren't just "extra" people; you are particularly special people. There are many things that only you can contribute. The family stories you know, the unique talents you have, the skills you've learned through the years . . . there are no replacements for those.

In the same way you try to see your grandchildren as unique individuals, you must try to realize that you, too, have a contribution that no one else can make and a place that no one else can fill. We are each essential, precious, useful.

So how do we work up to our own potential as grandparents? I'd suggest actually writing out your plan. If you are still employed, you'll have to set aside some of your leisure time to make your plan. If you are retired, you probably have filled your days with many other activities, so you, too, must find a time to make your plan. But do it soon.

The grandparent/grandchild connection is so vital, why not set aside some moments each week to improve it? Sometimes you may be actually *doing* things; other times you may be just doing your planning.

The Grandparent's Plan

You've been reading about being a grandparent. Now you need to start putting these ideas into practice. Some of the ideas in this book won't be pertinent to your situation. However, many of the ideas will be useful to you, so you must pick and choose which ones to try first.

Perhaps you'll want to start a file and add to it clippings on the subject of grandparenting, on gift ideas, on likely excursions, and on topics for discussion. This file will become your resource center for better communication and fun with your grandkids.

Next, make a list of things you learned from this book. Start with the idea of really getting to *know* your grandchildren. The quiz from page 14 of chapter 1 will give you some ideas. Then go back through the book and make note of other things you want to try. Your list might be like this:

1. I plan to get to know my grandchildren better through:
☐ Conversations when we're together.
☐ Weekly telephone calls.
☐ Setting up a telephone network among the grandchildren and bringing them together at our house.
☐ Regular by-mail communication of letters, postcards, and clippings.
☐ Worthwhile visits.
☐ Memorable celebrations.

2. I plan to share my talents with the grandchildren and other young people by:
☐ Making a list of those talents I can share.
☐ Talking with each grandchild about *one* of these.
☐ Working out a way to share my skill.
☐ Keeping the list, using it again and again.
☐ Using the file box idea on page 37 of chapter 2.
☐ Sharing skills with youth groups.

3. To help my grandchild appreciate our heritage, I will:
☐ Share photos and albums.
☐ Start a photo album for my grandchild.
☐ Outline and write a family history.
☐ Make a family tree.

☐ Put family stories on cassette.
☐ Make videos for far-away grandchildren.
☐ Visit an ethnic festival with the grandchildren.
☐ Take grandchildren to visit my old neighborhood.
☐ Start plans for a family reunion.

4. I plan to make my home a second home for our grandchildren. I can:
☐ Supply the house with interesting toys/games/books.
☐ Add variety of dinner menus and places (in the house) for us to eat.
☐ Include youngsters in mealtime conversation.
☐ Invite kids for overnight visits.
☐ Find private times to talk and share secrets.
☐ Investigate other opportunities to have the grandchildren and their friends enjoy our home.
☐ Make a list of odd-jobs grandkids can do with me so that they learn while helping.
☐ Make a list of odd-jobs they can do for pay.
☐ Try new recipes with the grandchildren's help.

5. I plan to enjoy our times together and build memories for us and our family by:
☐ Remembering to be flexible, happy, and creative.
☐ Finding something to praise in each grandchild.
☐ Recalling happy times from the past.
☐ Adding new ideas to the celebrations of family birthdays and other get-togethers.
☐ Starting new traditions for the family (see chapter 5, pages 82-83).
☐ Taking grandchildren on short trips, and longer ones if possible.

6. I plan to give the gifts of time and talent to my grandchildren, but when giving tangible gifts I will:
☐ Give equally to all grandchildren.
☐ Use books as gifts when possible.

☐ Ask grandkids for wish lists.

☐ Buy non-violent and long-lasting gifts.

☐ Consider buying one large gift for all the family rather than many small ones.

☐ When giving a money gift, also give a small wrapped gift.

☐ Encourage thank-you letters from grandchildren.

☐ Emphasize giving rather than receiving.

7. I plan to use creativity and love when I babysit or chaperon my grandchildren and to:

☐ Remember the parents' current aims for their kids.

☐ Use my authority gently.

☐ Try to be neither too strict nor too permissive.

☐ Learn effective methods of discipline and use them consistently.

☐ Encourage good traits of character.

☐ Originate a good three-generation discussion on obedience to family rules and the civil law.

☐ Assist the family in writing down some practical rules for living together.

☐ Help my children and grandchildren to live safely, keeping in mind the Grandparents' Workshop ideas at the end of chapter 7.

8. I plan to encourage my grandchildren to be responsible and to be appreciative of family values by:

☐ Learning about illegal and addictive substances and sharing my information.

☐ Emphasizing the difference between a good, moral, and happy life and a merely materialistic one lived in "the fast lane."

☐ Encouraging commitment to a complete education and training for a satisfying job.

☐ Stressing the merits of the marriage commitment.

☐ Setting an example of living a whole life, not one dominated by just work and television-viewing.

☐ Sharing my faith in God as a caring Parent and emphasizing what God has done and is doing for me.

☐ Instilling in my grandchildren the value of their own lives, the importance of life itself, and the opportunities ahead.

☐ Carrying my ideas into the community to help other young people.

9. I plan to be non-judgmental about my grandchildren and, rather than adding to their problems, to help them solve them by:

☐ Being alert to youth challenges and working with the parents.

☐ Being patient with those who are slower to learn or who have learning disabilities.

☐ Being unbending in my opposition to the use of drugs and alcohol and setting an example by abstaining from their use.

☐ Encouraging a wide variety of activities by not having the TV on when the family visits my house.

☐ Being willing to listen to the music my grandchildren like in return to their listening to my favorites.

☐ Not judging by appearance, but by the true substance of a grandchild and his friends.

☐ Living my own religion, letting my light shine, so that my family will also value what I value, but at the same time being willing to accept their own religious choices.

☐ Making politics an interesting discussion topic, not a heated debate.

☐ Accepting the spouses of my grandchildren with love and understanding.

10. I plan to let my grandchildren know I love them "no-matter-what" by:

☐ Speaking with kindness.

☐ Playing down sibling rivalry.

☐ Using the word *love* regularly.

☐ Giving hugs and kisses each time we're together.

☐ Writing of my love and interest when we're apart.

☐ Setting an example as a caring person.

☐ Sharing loving outreach with my grandchildren.

☐ Treating each grandchild with equal TLC.

☐ Going a step further and sharing my love with other children who need it.

11. **I plan to be creative in grandparenting by being willing to try new ideas.** (Reread chapter 11, "Grandma's Grab-bag," and see how many of these ideas are ones you can try.)

Making a Difference

In research I did for my book *Working Parent—Happy Child*, I found that almost 80 percent of parents felt that grandparents made a substantial contribution to the health and well-being of their children. They cited such qualities as love, patience, "being there," and listening.

Yes, listening is all-important. Kids get plenty of lectures nowadays, but not enough opportunities to talk with and to an attentive audience. That audience can be you, the grandparent. One of your special qualities is that you are *not* the parent. A grandchild can be very open and honest about feelings and problems with you. It's pivotal in your grandchild's experience to have a listening grandparent, a non-judgmental sounding board— one that won't tell all to the parent.

You can also make a difference by encouraging a good education. Start by teaching a child the love of books, then encouraging his ability to read. If a child can read well, he can do anything! Beyond making sure that your grandchild is literate (and you'd be amazed how many young people are not) encourage the *life-long* habits of reading books, taking classes, and learning how to do new things. Set an example by doing these things yourself.

The Costly Crunch of College

Paying for good schooling can be a giant task for parents. The average cost of just getting a child to age eighteen (food, clothing, share of housing, health care, education, and transportation) is well over one hundred thousand dollars. Now add to that the cost of college.

U. S. Department of Education statistics show that the cost of four years of college ranges from forty to one hundred thousand dollars. But statistics show that students with college degrees have lifetime earnings that are substantially more than those with only high school degrees. An advanced degree can double a starting salary.

While you aren't responsible for paying this (unless you choose to contribute in some way), you can understand that parents have a big financial load to carry. Your support of the parents' plans—whether moral, physical, prayerful, or financial—is essential.

Perhaps from your own experience in budgeting and saving, you can help parents plan ahead for college costs. That need seems so far away when children are toddlers—and there are so many more urgent needs for family funds. But advance planning can cut the costs down. Your biggest contribution to your grandchildren could be the information you share on how to pay for this costly expenditure.

Consider being the research person on this project. A little time spent talking with the financial officer at a few colleges and someone conversant in long-range saving plans can reap big dividends. Then, if you are able, you could make a donation to start a savings plan.

Looking Backward and Forward

When grandparents in my survey were asked what they remembered about their own grandparents, their recollections were of stern, reserved, yet loving people. This is why so many of these grandparents resolved to be more casual, more playful, less fussy. At the same time, they wanted to encourage some sense of organization, high expectations, and good educational goals for their grandchildren.

When your grandchildren look back on their times with you, what do you want them to remember? Having to behave at a long, boring dinner? Trying to be quiet while the adults talked? Or will those grandchildren remember your help in making a snow woman? Or staying up late to look at the stars? Or providing funny hats for everyone to wear at supper? Or bringing them a pizza during exam week? The memories are up to you to create.

As a grandparent, you can get away with things that the parent can't do. You can provide a welcome break in the daily schedule. You can be that original and grand person, the grandparent.

The grand qualities that make a grand grandparent are summed up in this double acrostic for the word *grandparent:*

GRACIOUSLY **G**IVING in a very personal way
RELIABLE **R**EMEMBRANCES of all the good of the past
AVAILABLE **A**LWAYS to help and comfort when needed
NEVER **N**EGATIVE and ever hopeful
DIRECTING **D**ILIGENTLY with both integrity and love
PATIENT and **P**OISED with mistakes and bad habits
AMUSING and **A**VAILABLE when times are hard and smiles
are needed
RESPONSIBLE and **R**ELEVANT as a role model for honest,
joyful living in today's world
EAGER and **E**ASY about sharing talents and good ideas
NATURAL and **N**ORMAL in response to youth's
  sometimes startling ideas
TRUTHFUL but **T**ACTFUL about moral and ethical values
SPECIAL and **S**PECTACULAR in ways of showing love

That's you . . . so go onward from here!

To close, I'd like to share what a grandmother felt when holding her first grandchild:

"It was almost more exciting than having my own babies, for I already knew some of the wonderful things ahead for this little one. Her hand curled around mine, wanting to hang on tightly to me, a part of her past and a part of her future.

"When she cried, it was little soft sounds, as if she knew the challenges ahead: times for tears of sadness and tears of joy. Her tiny chin quivered as if not quite sure there would be hands to help and love to comfort. Was it going to be all right? I told her, 'Yes!'

"Those dark eyes looked up, seeing and unseeing, trying to focus on what was real and what was not. Were they asking me what was important and would make a difference—and what was trivial and didn't matter? I told her those decisions would come in good time, and that her parents and I would be there to guide.

"All dressed in layers of lacy frills, she was like a rosebud about to open. Yes, life wouldn't be all frilly party dresses, there would be work clothes and play clothes and jeans and jammies. Oh, the many outfits this little body would wear! But these clothes would be just the outward trappings of her inward soul, forever one of God's children, for a while entrusted to her parents' care.

"Oh, little one, you will soon know I'm your grandparent. How I treasure the moments ahead as I watch over you!"

Books on Grandparenting

Books for you to fill in for your grandchildren

Grandmother Remembers: A Written Heirloom for My Grandchild, Judith
  Levy and Judy Peliken (Stewart, Tabori and Chang)
Grandmother's Book, H. L. Levin (Crown, 1987)
Grandparent's Journal, A Keepsake Book with Space for Notes (Running
  Press)

Other books about grandparenting

Grandparenting, David A. Elkins (Scott Foresman, 1990)
Grandparents, Grandchildren: The Vital Connection, Arthur Kornhaber
  (Transaction Pub., 1981)
Mum's the Word: The Wit and Wisdom of a Semi-Sweet Grandmother, Evelyn
  Abrahams (Price Stern, 1985)
The New American Grandparent: A Place in the Family, a Life Apart, Andrew
  Cherlin and J. T. Furstenberg (Basic, 1986)
*The Grandparents Book: The Joys and Frustrations of Coping with Your
  Offspring's Offspring,* Anastazia Little and Stuart Little (Slawson
  Comm., 1988)
Grandparents: A Special Kind of Love, Eda LeShan (Macmillan, 1984)
How to Grandparent, Fitzhugh Dodson (Harper & Row, 1981)
*Instant Parent: A Guide for Step-Parents, Part-time Parents, and
  Grandparents,* Suzy Kalter (A & W, 1979, 1989)
Funny, You Don't Look Like a Grandmother, Lois Wyse (Crown, 1989)
Grandma Knows Best, But No One Ever Listens, Mary McBride
  (Meadowbrook, 1987)

Good books on parenting to recommend to your children:

How to Raise Good Children, Laurel Hughes (Abingdon Press, 1985)
Understanding Your School-Aged Child (Time-Life, 1988)
Working Parent—Happy Child, Caryl Krueger (Abingdon Press, 1990)
Parenting Isn't For Cowards, James Dobson (Word Books, 1987)
Parent Effectiveness Training: The Tested Way to Raise Respectable Children,
    Thomas Gordon (NAL, 1988)
1001 Things to Do with Your Kids, Caryl Krueger (Abingdon Press, 1988)
Your Gifted Child, Joan Franklin Smutny, Kathleen Veenker, and Stephen
    Veenker (Facts on File, 1989)

Storybooks about grandparents:

The Berenstain Bears and the Week at Grandma's, Stan Berenstain and
    Janice Berenstain (Random, 1986)
Grandmother's Tales, Celia Berridge (Deutsch, 1982)
Nana Upstairs and Nana Downstairs, Tomi De Paola (Putnam, 1973)
Grandmother Is Someone Special, Susan Goldman (Whitman, 1976)
Grandad's Place, Helen Griffith (Greenwillow, 1987)
I Dance in My Red Pajamas, Edith Hurd (Harper, 1982)
Luke's Garden and Gramp, Joan Tate (HarpJ, 1981)
Can You Hear Me Grandad? Pat Thomson (Dell, 1988)
Good Girl Granny, Pat Thomson (Dell, 1988)
Happy Birthday, Grandpa, Harriet Ziefert (Harper, 1988)
With Love from Grandma, Harriet Ziefert (Penguin, 1989)